FOOD FOREST
BIBLE

Samuel D. Livingston

Table of Content

INTRODUCTION..5

CHAPTER 1

WHY SHOULD YOU CREATE YOUR OWN FOOD FOREST...... ...10

Benefits of a food forest...2

CHAPTER 2

FOUNDATIONAL KNOWLEDGE OF A FOOD FOREST 15

What is a food forest...15

How you can start your own food forest...............................15

Principles of a food forest design...17

Comparison between food forest and traditional agriculture....................18

Food forest flexible and sustainable resource......................19

CHAPTER 3

SITE SELECTION, PREPARATION AND DESIGN...........................21

Land assessment and design...................,...........................21

Determine if swales are a viable water management option for your terrains...............,..25

Soil health and regeneration...................................,..............30

Reducing waste using a closed loop system...............,..........41

Design principles of a food forest.................,......................43

Implementing a climate resilient food forest...............,.......46

Design patterns...............,..47

Design diversity and edge effect...................,.......................50

CHAPTER 4

PLANT SELECTION AND CARE................,..55

Choosing the right Plants.............,...59

Plant guild and companion systems............,..................................~77

Best companion plant combinations.............,.................................~79

CHAPTER 5

PLANTING AND PROPAGATION.............,....................................83

Seed starting...............,...85

Grafting ....,...~91

Cuttings..............,.............. 96

Planting techniques and spacing,...104

Transplanting and aftercare.... ....,.................................~09

CHAPTER 6

FOOD FOREST MANAGEMENT

The fungal layer.............,...114

Maximizing the fungal layer....~............,......................................116

Pruning and care.............,...122

Pest and disease control..............,...128

Fertilization and soil amendment............,...................................134

Soil amendment...........,..139

Water management...........,...141

Attracting beneficial insects.............,...150

CHAPTER 7

FOREST SUCCESSION..............,...165

The basics of ecological succession.................,..............................165

Stages of succession in a food forest.............,.............................168

Designing food forest with succession in mind............,.................185

Ecological benefits of natural succession in a food forest,.............188

Managing succession in a food forest..191

CHAPTER 8

FOREST GARDENING SYSTEMS...............,..............................195

Food forest models.............,..199

Woodlands and forest gardens.............,...209

CHAPTER 9

DEVELOPING A MAINTENANCE PLAN............,...........................214

Seasonal task and observations.................,.................................221

No-Till gardening.............,..225

CHAPTER 10

HARVESTING AND PRESERVATION.............,.............................231

Harvesting.............,..231

Food preservation............,...237

CONCLUSION.............,..248

INTRODUCTION

Imagine standing beneath the sweeping branches of a hundred-year-old apple tree, planted by your great-grandfather, its gnarled roots gripping the earth as firmly as your own family history. The fruits that dangle above, ripening under the sun, are not just apples. They're stories, nourished by generations of care, knowledge, and dedication to the land. That apple tree—and the entire ecosystem around it—is part of a food forest that began long before you were born and will continue to flourish long after you're gone. This is the legacy my great-grandfather left for me, a thriving, self-sustaining forest that has fed, sheltered, and inspired our family for generations. And as I write this, I'm here to tell you that you, too, can build this kind of legacy—a food forest that will provide nourishment, resilience, and an enduring gift to the generations that follow.

When my great-grandfather began planting the first layers of our food forest, he had no idea the impact it would have on the lives of those who would follow. But he did know one thing: he wanted to create something that lasted, something that could feed his family beyond his own lifetime. Over the years, that humble vision evolved into an abundant, layered ecosystem, filled with fruit trees, shrubs, vines, ground covers, and root vegetables, all woven together into a natural tapestry. Through the years, each member of our family has played a part in maintaining and expanding this food forest. Today, I'm honored to carry forward what he began, and I am committed to passing down not just the land itself, but the knowledge and practices needed to sustain it. In many ways, this book is an extension of that commitment—a guide to help you start, nurture, and eventually bequeath a living ecosystem that will serve as a source of food, wonder, and resilience for generations to come.

A food forest, at its core, is a way to secure your family's food independence. In an age where food systems are increasingly vulnerable—disrupted by climate change, supply chain instability, and market fluctuations—a food forest provides an unshakable foundation of self-reliance. When you cultivate a diverse ecosystem filled with edible plants, medicinal herbs, and soil-enriching ground covers, you're not only creating food security, you're crafting a landscape that requires less labor, fewer chemical inputs, and no dependency on outside sources for nutrition. You're investing in an agricultural system that can handle the uncertainties of the future. You're growing in abundance, even in the face of adversity.

My great-grandfather understood this, even in his time. While he may not have used terms like "resilience" or "sustainability," he knew that working with nature rather than against it would yield lasting rewards. Our food forest has thrived through droughts, storms, and the gradual urbanization of the surrounding areas. While farms in our region suffered during certain seasons, our food forest continued to provide—its diversity acting as a natural buffer against climate impacts. This is why a food forest isn't just a garden; it's a legacy that is built to withstand the tests of time.

But a food forest is much more than a safeguard. It's an immersive, living library of knowledge and tradition. Growing up in this forest taught me things that I could never have learned in a classroom. I learned which plants grow best together, how certain shrubs could deter pests naturally, and how to harvest without disrupting the surrounding ecosystem. Each plant, from the towering fruit trees to the tiniest ground covers, plays a role. By planting in layers—canopy, understory, shrubs, herbs, ground covers, vines, and roots—our food forest operates as a complex, self-sustaining organism, where each layer supports the others. My great-grandfather's wisdom, passed down through my grandfather and father, is encoded in this ecosystem, and it's the same knowledge I am eager to pass along to you in these pages.

Imagine building a legacy for your own family that, one day, your great-grandchildren can inherit. Imagine them stepping into an orchard filled with the trees you planted, the same way I step into the one my great-grandfather began. They'll learn from the same natural world that taught you and draw nourishment from the food forest you carefully designed. And they'll find sustenance in something far beyond the harvest—it's in the stories, the pride, and the sense of responsibility that come with inheriting a thriving ecosystem. That is what a food forest offers; it's a way of nurturing not only the land but also the bonds between generations.

In writing this guide, I've drawn deeply from my family's experience. This book is not merely a collection of gardening techniques or ecological theory; it is a testament to the value of working alongside nature to build something meaningful and lasting. Each chapter is designed to empower you to create a food forest that can thrive independently—one that doesn't require constant labor, but rather develops its own resilience over time. You'll learn how to build rich soil, how to plant according to natural succession, and how to harness the symbiotic relationships between plants to boost productivity. You'll also learn about practical issues: choosing the right plants for your climate, designing for both efficiency and beauty, and troubleshooting common challenges that arise in forest gardening.

A food forest is one of the greatest investments you can make in the future of your family. Not only does it yield fresh, nutrient-rich food season after season, it also reduces reliance on grocery stores and packaged food. It offers a year-round pantry that is resilient, organic, and truly home-grown. And as you cultivate your food forest, you're not only feeding your family today; you're preserving biodiversity, fostering ecological health, and creating a landscape that will mature and thrive over time.

For my family, the food forest has been a source of peace, purpose, and prosperity. It's where we gather to celebrate the changing seasons, to share meals, and to teach each new generation about the land. In today's world, where so much of our food comes from faraway farms and industrialized systems, a food forest represents an act of defiance—a return to simplicity, sustainability, and independence. As you read this book and begin your own journey, I encourage you to think beyond the present moment. Think of the family members you may never meet, who will one day walk beneath the trees you plant. Think of the taste of fresh fruit and vegetables, grown from a system that doesn't require synthetic inputs or fossil fuels. And think of the wisdom you'll gain, which you too can pass down as part of your own family's story.

In the following pages, I hope to inspire you with the knowledge and vision needed to create a thriving, abundant food forest. My great-grandfather's legacy endures in the leaves, roots, and fruits of the forest he began, and my goal is to help you plant a legacy of your own—one that will nourish, protect, and enrich the lives of your loved ones for generations to come. In embarking on this journey, you're not merely planting a garden. You're making a statement about the kind of world you want to leave behind: one of resilience, abundance, and deep connection to the natural world. Let this book be your guide, and may your food forest be as enduring and fruitful as the legacy I am privileged to carry forward.

CHAPTER ONE

WHY SHOULD YOU CREATE YOUR OWN FOOD FOREST

Food security has always been at the heart of human civilization. The ongoing challenge of feeding an ever-growing population is a task that farmers, scientists, and policymakers are dedicated to tackling every single day. Creating a food forest is a visionary investment in a sustainable future, offering a wide range of benefits that will resonate for generations to come. By designing and nurturing a food forest, you're building a climate-resilient ecosystem that preserves biodiversity, maintains soil health, and provides a stable source of nutritious food. This, in turn, fosters food security, supports healthy lifestyles, and encourages a deep connection with nature. A mature food forest can also appreciate property value, generate income, and reduce reliance on external food sources, ensuring economic benefits. Moreover, it serves as a living classroom for hands-on learning about ecology, botany, and sustainable living, allowing you to pass down valuable knowledge and cultural heritage to future generations. Ultimately, a food forest is a legacy of abundance, weaving together environmental stewardship, nutritional well-being, economic resilience, and educational enrichment for a brighter, more sustainable future.

One effective approach to enhancing local food security on a smaller scale is the creation of food forests. Unlike traditional gardens, food forests are intricate, self-sustaining ecosystems brimming with a variety of food-producing plants. They offer a robust source of nourishment, demanding minimal upkeep while fostering biodiversity and enriching soil health. These man-made food forests draw inspiration from natural forests, designed by Mother Nature herself, which flourish without human intervention, teeming with life and sustainability.

This food forest used to be our front lawn. Now it's a place filled with abundance for people, plants and wildlife. Planting a food forest is one way to help heal our living world

Whereas gardens are often a single layer of vegetables, food forests mimic the multi-layered structure of natural forests, creating a rich, diverse ecosystem. Typically, a food forest comprises seven layers, although smaller versions can function effectively with fewer layers. These layers include the canopy of large fruit and nut trees, an understory of dwarf fruit trees, shrubs like blueberries or currants, herbaceous perennials, a soil surface covered with crops such as creeping thyme, root crops in the soil/rhizosphere, and a vertical layer of climbing vines. This structure enables food forests to maximize space and productivity, creating a sustainable and resilient food source.

The biodiversity in food forests helps solve many issues faced in traditional gardening and agriculture. For example, food forests attract beneficial insects that prey on pests, reducing the need for pesticides and minimizing plant damage. This biodiversity also attracts pollinators like bees and butterflies, crucial for the healthy reproduction of many crops. Food forests offer significant environmental benefits, such as carbon sequestration. Due to their high plant diversity and density, food forests can sequester more carbon than traditional forests. Additionally, by growing food locally, they reduce the need for transportation and storage, thereby helping mitigate climate change. Water conservation is another advantage of food forests. The deep roots of trees and shrubs retain soil moisture, lessening the need for irrigation. The variety of plants also helps prevent erosion and improve soil health, further reducing water usage.

Socially, food forests foster community building and education. They provide a space for community members to learn about sustainable agriculture, share knowledge, and build relationships. Food forests also offer educational opportunities about nutrition, healthy eating, food preparation, and preservation. Economically, food forests can boost development by providing income for farmers and small-scale producers. They produce a wide range of crops, such as fruits, nuts, vegetables, and herbs, which can be sold locally or used to make value-added products like jams. Furthermore, food forests can promote ecotourism, generating income for local communities.

THE BENEFITS OF A FOOD FOREST

Starting a food forest or garden offers numerous benefits. Food forests prioritize the health of trees, perennials, shrubs, and other self-seeding plants by employing dense planting techniques and soil covers to prevent weeds. They also use indirect plants, such as nitrogen-fixers and mineral accumulators, to attract beneficial insects that control pests without pesticides, which can harm plants and the environment. These plants enhance the resilience of crops, reducing the need for chemicals and fertilizers, which helps lower emissions. Food forests operate in harmony with nature, similar to climate-smart farming, requiring minimal upkeep and resembling natural gardens. Besides their environmental and harvest advantages, food forests are visually appealing.

The plant diversity in a food forest attracts a wide range of insects that aid in pollination and deter pests. It also utilizes the natural terrain to maximize rainwater collection, providing a sustainable water resource for all plants. Additionally, the strategic design of a food forest can protect crops from unexpected weather conditions, such as strong winds. A key advantage of a food forest is its ability to self-replenish once established, eliminating the need for annual replanting. While some animals like deer or rabbits may eat certain herbs, most species find the food forest's produce unappealing or inaccessible, such as mushrooms growing in tree crevices. Even if some plants are disturbed, the regenerative setup of a food forest allows for quick regrowth.

CHAPTER TWO

FOUNDATIONAL KNOWLEDGE OF A FOOD FOREST

WHAT IS A FOOD FOREST

A food forest, also referred to as a forest garden, is a cultivation approach that mimics the natural growth patterns of ecosystems to optimize crop yields. This innovative method involves designing a three-dimensional landscape where plants thrive in all directions - upwards, downwards, and outwards - much like the sprawling branches of a tree or the unfolding petals of a flower, creating a lush and productive environment.

Envision a food forest as a vibrant tapestry of diverse plants, much like a garden filled with a variety of flowers. Just as a mix of flowers enhances beauty and biodiversity, a food forest thrives on the synergy of multiple plant species. By growing a range of fruits, vegetables, and edible plants together, you create a dynamic ecosystem that offers numerous benefits. For example, pollinators like bees are drawn to specific flowers, but by planting these alongside other complementary species, you increase the chances of successful pollination. Similarly, a food forest's diverse array of plants fosters a richer nutritional profile and supports healthier growth, making it a more resilient and productive approach than cultivating a single crop in isolation.

HOW YOU CAN START YOUR OWN FOOD FOREST

Starting a food forest in your backyard is accessible to anyone, but it requires careful planning and consideration. Begin by deciding which types of food you want to grow and identifying the necessary plants and herbs for a self-sustaining ecosystem. Climate is a crucial factor, as some crops may not thrive year-round in certain regions. Choose a location with ample space, ideally with existing trees, and assess your surroundings, including local wildlife, natural soil growth, and potential pests. Create a sketch of your food forest design, weighing the pros and cons of your chosen site. Next, prepare your soil for long-term fertility using techniques like soil moderation, amendments, or the "lasagna method" - layering cardboard, wood chips, and manure to facilitate decomposition. With these steps, you'll be well on your way to creating a thriving food forest that requires minimal maintenance.

The next step in creating a food forest is to establish the canopy layer, ideally using existing tall trees or planting fruit trees like cherry or plum trees. This layer provides shade and structure for the rest of the forest. The understory layer comes next, featuring berry bushes or other shrubs that thrive in partial shade, planted in a direction that maximizes sunlight. The herbaceous layer consists of herbs like rosemary, mint, and thyme, which benefit from the shade provided by the understory layer. Additional small plants like lettuces, edible flowers, or beans can be added to provide further shade and diversity. Optional but beneficial are vining plants like potatoes, squashes, or grapes, which can ensure a year-round harvest. Remember that growing a food forest is a process of experimentation and adaptation, and the first year may not yield perfect results. However, with time and patience, a food forest can lead to cost savings, reduced plastic use, and lower emissions, making it a rewarding and sustainable endeavor.

PRINCIPLES OF FOOD FOREST DESIGN

A food forest is a deliberately designed ecosystem that replicates the natural forest's structure and function, with the added benefit of producing a diverse array of edible plants. To achieve this, three core principles guide its creation: imitating nature's diversity, harmonious grouping, and planning for evolution. By embracing diversity, food forests foster a thriving ecosystem where various species coexist and support each other, unlike monoculture farming. This diversity is further enhanced by harmonious grouping, where plants are intentionally combined in beneficial relationships, such as pairing nitrogen-fixing plants with fruit trees to enrich the soil. Finally, understanding the natural succession of plant life in an area informs the design of the food forest, ensuring that plants are selected to flourish at different stages of the forest's growth and development, ultimately creating a resilient and productive ecosystem.

While creating your own food forest, prioritize efficiency and sustainability through a harmonious combination of three key strategies. By focusing on perennial plants, the need for frequent planting and maintenance is significantly reduced, allowing for a more self-sufficient system. This self-sufficiency is further enhanced by closed-loop systems, where nutrients and water are continually cycled back into the system, minimizing the need for external resources like fertilizers and water. At the heart of this approach is soil regeneration, where techniques like composting, cover cropping, and minimal soil disturbance are used to create a fertile and thriving soil ecosystem. As these strategies work together, they create a highly efficient and sustainable food forest that requires minimal external inputs, produces a diverse array of edible plants, and fosters a resilient and regenerative environment.

Food forests also embody two key benefits which are diversity and resilience. By incorporating multiple layers of plant growth, from towering trees to low-lying ground cover, they optimize space usage. The intersection of different plant communities, known as edge effects, boosts biodiversity and productivity. This diverse ecosystem, comprising a wide array of plants and animals, fosters resilience against pests and diseases. Furthermore, food forests contribute to human well-being by providing food security through a sustainable harvest, creating habitats for wildlife and pollinators, and offering opportunities for education, recreation, and connection with nature. A well-designed food forest requires a site-specific approach, taking into account local climate, soil conditions, and available space to create a unique and thriving ecosystem. This tailored design enables efficient water management, harnessing and retaining water effectively to support optimal plant growth. Furthermore, careful planning and design minimize energy inputs, ensuring energy efficiency and promoting sustainability. By integrating these elements, a food forest can achieve a harmonious balance between nature and human needs, fostering a resilient and productive environment that requires minimal external resources.

COMPARISON BETWEEN A FOOD FOREST WITH TRADITIONAL AGRICULTURE

Food forests and traditional agriculture represent two fundamentally different approaches to food production, with distinct priorities and outcomes. Traditional agriculture focuses on short-term gains, relying on monoculture, annual crops, and heavy chemical inputs, which can lead to soil depletion and erosion. In contrast, food forests prioritize long-term sustainability, employing polyculture, perennial plants, and natural pest control to create a resilient ecosystem. By building soil health through composting and minimal disturbance, food forests reduce labor and increase biodiversity, promoting a balanced and thriving environment. While traditional agriculture relies heavily on mechanization and chemical inputs, food forests emphasize manual labor and natural processes, resulting in a more sustainable and diverse food system. Ultimately, traditional agriculture seeks to maximize yields in a single season, whereas food forests aim to create a regenerative ecosystem that provides food and benefits for generations to come.

FOOD FOREST FLEXIBLE AND SUSTAINABLE RESOURCES

Food forests are flexible and sustainable systems that thrive by leveraging a diverse range of resources, including natural resources like sunlight, water, soil, and biodiversity, which are optimized through design and management. Human resources, such as knowledge, labor, and creativity, are essential for designing, planting, and maintaining these systems, while infrastructure elements like fencing, paths, and structures support access and productivity. Renewable resources, including compost, mulch, and solar power, minimize external inputs, and social resources like community support and education foster a supportive network. By embracing flexibility, sustainability, and resilience, food forests can adapt to various scales and conditions, promoting long-term ecological balance, climate change mitigation, and abundant food production, ultimately becoming thriving ecosystems that provide numerous benefits.

Fresh coffee harvest from my food forest

CHAPTER THREE

SITE SELECTION, PREPARATION AND DESIGN

Next, think about your property's soil type

Trees like almond, fig, and olive thrive in areas with full sun and good drainage, while hazelnut, mulberry, and apple trees prefer partial shade and moist soil. For areas with steep slopes, chestnut and elderberry trees are suitable due to their strong root systems and adaptability to various soil conditions. In cold climates, crabapple and birch trees are hardy and adaptable options. However, it's essential to consider additional factors such as root systems, wind exposure, and pollinators when planting, and to research the specific requirements of each tree species to ensure compatibility with your land's conditions. Always carefully select tree species based on your land's unique characteristics.

Soil analysis

A comprehensive soil analysis will provide invaluable insights into its composition, fertility, and potential limitations. Analyzing key soil properties is necessary for understanding its potential to support plant growth. Soil texture, which determines water and air movement, can range from sandy (quick-draining but nutrient-poor) to clay (water-retentive but prone to compaction) to loamy (ideally balanced for good drainage and nutrient retention). Soil structure, referring to the arrangement of particles, should be crumbly to allow for air and water movement, as clumpy or compacted soil hinders root growth. Soil pH, measuring acidity or alkalinity, should fall between 6.0-7.0 for optimal plant growth, as acidic or alkaline conditions can limit nutrient availability or uptake. Organic matter content, indicating soil fertility and water-holding capacity, should be high to improve soil structure, nutrient retention, and water infiltration. Finally, nutrient levels, including essential macronutrients like nitrogen, phosphorus, and potassium, as well as micronutrients like calcium, magnesium, and iron, must be assessed to ensure optimal plant growth. By understanding these interconnected soil properties, you can tailor your soil management strategies to create a fertile and supportive environment for your plants.

Debris from land cover serves as compost and mulch

Conducting a soil analysis is an important step in understanding your soil's needs and creating a thriving garden. Let's start with a visual inspection, where you observe soil color, texture, and structure, looking for signs of compaction, erosion, or poor drainage. Next, you can use home soil test kits for a basic understanding of pH and nutrient levels, or send your soil to a professional laboratory for a comprehensive analysis. It's time to analyze your results once you receive them! If your soil has a low pH, you'll need to add lime to increase it. This can be done by irrigating the soil with lime water. If it's too high, apply sulfur to lower it.

Soil test kit

If your soil lacks organic matter, incorporate compost, manure, or cover crops. And if you find nutrient deficiencies, apply specific fertilizers based on your test results. Building soil health is an ongoing process, regardless of your soil's initial condition. Focus on improving soil health through composting, which adds organic matter to enhance soil structure and fertility. Use cover cropping to protect soil, prevent erosion, and add organic matter. Practice crop rotation to prevent soil depletion, and mulch to protect soil from erosion, retain moisture, and suppress weeds.

Water availability

Water is a critical component for the success of any food forest. By understanding your region's water patterns and implementing efficient water management strategies, you can ensure the health and productivity of your ecosystem. Start by analyzing your region's rainfall patterns, including annual totals, seasonal variations, and intensity. Next, identify potential water sources like ponds, rivers, or wells, and assess your soil's ability to hold water, recognizing that sandy soils drain quickly while clay soils retain water more effectively. To maximize water availability, consider implementing water harvesting and storage strategies like rainwater harvesting, where you collect and direct rainwater from rooftops to water-holding features like ponds, cisterns, or rain gardens. Also create swales to capture and slow down rainwater runoff, allowing it to infiltrate the soil, and apply a thick layer of mulch to help retain soil moisture. Consider creating a pond or water feature to store rainwater for irrigation or as a habitat for aquatic life.

To achieve efficient water use, it's essential to adopt a holistic approach that incorporates multiple strategies. Begin by selecting drought-tolerant plants that are well-suited to your region's climate, and apply a thick layer of mulch to reduce evaporation and maintain soil moisture. Consider using drip irrigation systems for targeted water delivery to plant roots, and group plants with similar water needs together in water-wise landscaping designs.

However, efficient water use goes beyond these measures. Healthy soil, achieved through composting and cover cropping, has better water-holding capacity, while a diverse range of plants with different water requirements can help ensure water availability throughout the year. Finally, regularly monitoring soil moisture levels allows you to adjust watering practices as needed.

DETERMINE IF SWALES ARE A VIABLE WATER MANAGEMENT OPTION FOR YOUR TERRAIN

When considering whether swales are suitable for your terrain, it's important to understand their purpose and the specific conditions that affect their effectiveness. Swales are contour ditches designed to capture and gradually release rainwater, which helps to reduce runoff and improve soil moisture. This makes them a valuable tool for managing water in food forests, but their success depends on several key factors related to your land. First, examine the **slope** of your terrain. Swales work best on gentle to moderate slopes, typically those less than 15%. On steeper slopes, additional erosion control measures, such as terraces, may be necessary to prevent soil loss. While swales can also be used on flat land, their effectiveness may be reduced in such settings. Next, think about your property's soil type. Swales are most effective in permeable soils, which allow water to infiltrate easily. However, if your soil is predominantly clay, which has poor drainage, you may need to integrate swales with other water management techniques to achieve the desired results.

Rainfall patterns in your area also play a crucial role. In regions with high rainfall, swales can help prevent erosion and manage excess water, while in low-rainfall areas, they can be valuable for capturing and storing water for use during dry periods. The presence of **existing vegetation** should not be overlooked. Dense vegetation naturally slows down water runoff, which might reduce the need for extensive swales. In contrast, less vegetated areas may benefit more from swales to control water flow and prevent erosion.

To determine if swales are right for your terrain, start with a **visual inspection** of your land to observe slope, soil conditions, and water flow patterns. **Topographic maps** can help you understand the contours of your land, and **soil testing** will give you insights into the soil's water-holding capacity. You'll need to consider factors such as **swale spacing**—which should be based on your land's slope and soil type—and **swale depth,** ensuring it captures enough water without hindering plant growth. Regular maintenance swales are essential to prevent sediment buildup and ensure they continue to function properly.

If your land has a gentle to moderate slope and permeable soil, swales are likely a suitable option. However, for more complex terrains or challenging soil conditions, you may need to combine swales with other water management strategies, such as ponds, cisterns, or rain gardens, to achieve the best results. Verifying the slopes on your property is a straightforward process that can be completed in just 5 minutes using the Google Earth desktop application, eliminating the need for manual assessments or smartphone apps.

Step 1: Launch Google Earth, then find your property

Explore your property's slopes from the comfort of your own space! Simply use Google Earth's search function to virtually 'fly over' your land, enter your address, and zoom in to visualize the slopes without having to physically visit the site.

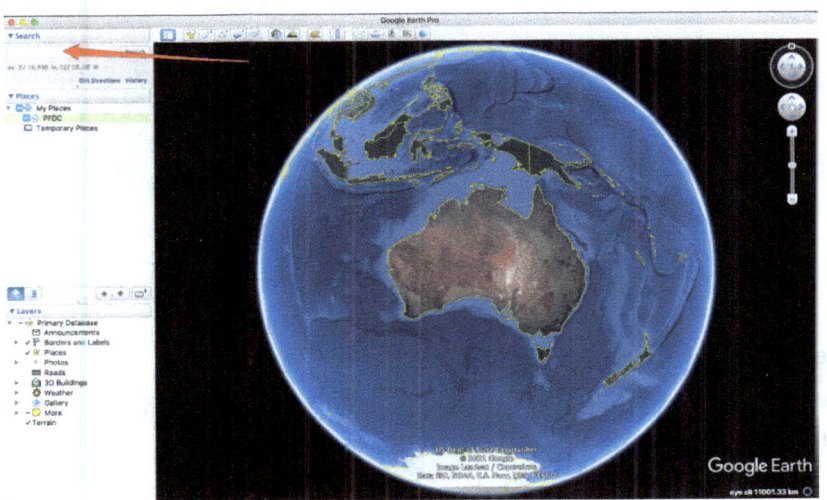

Arrow shows search area

Step 2: Draw a straight line with a ruler

Use Google Earth to navigate and zoom in on the area, getting a sense of the slope's orientation. This will help you determine the optimal direction to analyze it. First, click on the 'Ruler' tool in the toolbar (step 1) and then switch to the 'Path' tab (step 2). Next, draw a straight line across your property (step 3). This will help you visualize and measure the slope, making it easier to understand your land's layout.

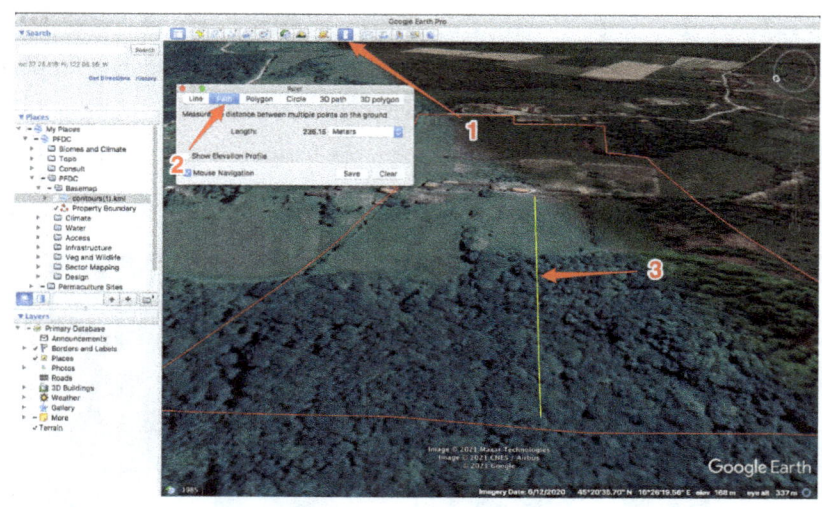

Step 3: Show elevation profile

Check the 'show elevation profile' option to show the elevation profile of the path you just drew.

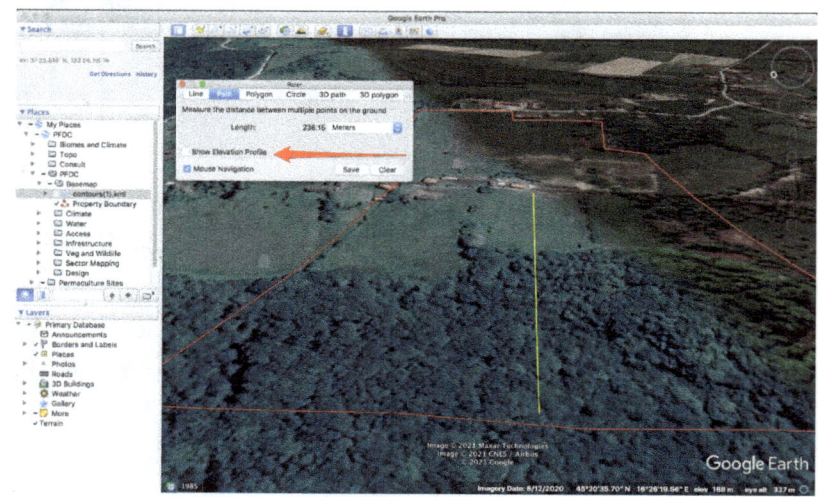

Step 4: Assess the slope

As you hover your mouse over the elevation profile, notice the red arrow that appears on the map, indicating the exact location. You'll also see important details displayed, including the height above sea level and the gradient at that specific point. Be sure to check the 'avg slope' value, which will give you a clear understanding of the slope's steepness, helping you assess the landscape's incline and make informed decisions.

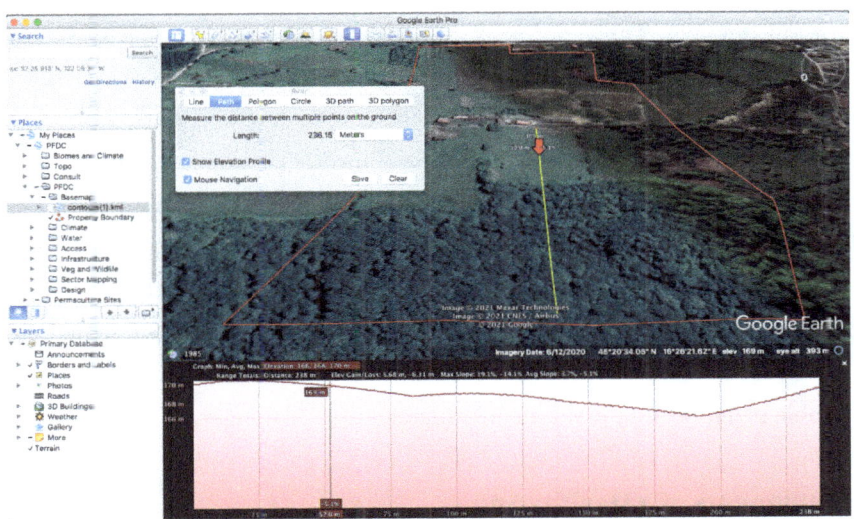

Note: If the elevation profile is too short to display the average slope value, don't worry! You can easily calculate it manually using the formula: (Rise ÷ Run) x 100. For instance, if the elevation gain or loss (rise) is 15 meters and the distance (run) is 200 meters, simply plug in the numbers: (15 ÷ 200) x 100 = 7.5%. This will give you the percentage slope value, helping you understand the terrain's incline.

Having accurately assessed your slope using these methods, you'll now be able to determine if it meets the 15% slope requirement. If it does, you'll have the flexibility to install swales in various locations throughout the area, wherever they're needed, giving you the freedom to design and implement your water harvesting system with confidence.

SOIL HEALTH AND REGENERATION

When cultivating food, we often overlook the vibrant ecosystem thriving beneath our feet. The well-being of our plants is deeply connected to the complex network of soil life, mycelium, roots, and natural elements - known as the 'Wood Wide Web'. The key to creating a resilient and self-sufficient food-growing system "food forests" is improving soil health through nurturing these relationships. Soil health is the foundation of our food, and its vitality directly impacts the health of our crops. Soil is a living entity that breathes, consumes, and grows, requiring nutrition to support plant ecosystems. Just like living beings, soil needs essential nutrients to thrive. Let's explore the key nutritional elements that make soil fertile and capable of supporting plant life, distinguishing it from mere dirt.

Components of a Healthy Soil
Vitamin Water

Although water isn't technically a vitamin, it is essential for the survival of all life forms, infusing life into everything it touches. A large portion of the Earth and its inhabitants is composed of water, making it accurate to say that soil and water are inseparable partners. Therefore, it's essential for soil to have water, as its absence can dry out the soil, rendering it uninhabitable for life. Water also acts as a solvent for other soil nutrients, helping them move from one place to another.

Organic Matter

Decomposing materials like fallen leaves, vegetable scraps, dead animals, insects, and animal waste contribute to the nitrogen, phosphorus, and sulfur levels in the soil. Ideally, soil should contain 3-5% carbon content, with this organic matter forming the soil's humus.

Air

Air is another vital element for life. Many organisms, including humans, depend on air for oxygen. A similar process occurs underground, where airflow is crucial for delivering oxygen to soil microorganisms. About 50% of the soil's volume consists of air pores, which contain oxygen, carbon dioxide, nitrogen, and water vapor—essential gasses for the survival of soil's microbial life. As these microbes respire, they release carbon dioxide, making it vital for the soil to be well-aerated to allow oxygen in and carbon dioxide out.

Living Organisms

All living creatures—such as insects, worms, bacteria, algae, and more—make up the 'soil food web,' highlighting the strong interconnectedness of life below the soil's surface. According to the US Department of Agriculture, a teaspoon of soil can contain 100 million to 1 billion microbes, including fungi, bacteria, algae, protozoa, worms, arthropods, and nematodes. Soil that is fertile and suitable for agriculture typically has a higher concentration of these microbes than non-agricultural land.

Minerals

Just as minerals are essential for human nutrition, they are also crucial for plant nutrition. While farmers often focus on boosting nitrogen and carbon content in the soil due to their significant health benefits, other minerals, which are sometimes overlooked, also play an important role in improving soil health. All essential minerals work together to collectively enhance soil quality.

The touch and feel of a healthy soil

A healthy soil structure relies on three key components: sand, silt, and clay. However, none of these elements alone can support a robust plant system, which is why you typically see people lounging on sandy beaches and statues crafted from clay, rather than growing plants in such materials.

For effective food-growing systems, these components must work in harmony.

- **Sand:** creates larger pores in the soil, allowing for proper air circulation.
- **Silt:** retains water efficiently and forms smaller pores.
- **Clay:** excels at holding water and nutrients but doesn't facilitate air circulation well.

The right balance of these three elements results in a soil structure that is loose, friable (easily crumbled with little pressure), and capable of draining water effectively. This combination produces what is known as "loamy" soil, which is considered ideal for plant growth. Loamy soil is highly fertile, composed of a mix of clay, sand, silt, and organic matter. It retains ample moisture while still draining well, ensuring that water reaches the plant roots without causing overwatering, making it perfect for cultivation.

How to check soil health

Start by visually inspecting your plants. Are they growing as expected, or do you notice issues like stunted growth or rotting? Healthy plants are typically a sign of healthy soil. Next, check for water drainage. Soil that drains well is a positive indicator, whereas water stagnation is undesirable and can suggest problems with the soil.

Also, pay attention to the presence of earthworms and other insects, as their presence indicates a thriving soil ecosystem. Healthy soil naturally attracts these beneficial organisms, and their activity is a good sign. Finally, assess how easy it is to work with the soil. Is it friable, meaning it crumbles easily, or is it lumpy and rocky? The ease with which you can handle the soil reflects its structural health.

Examining your soil: How to test for nutrient content and texture

Soil testing is a vital diagnostic tool for your food forest, offering a comprehensive understanding of your soil's composition and guiding informed decisions on soil enhancements and plant care. By identifying nutrient levels, you can tailor your approach to meet specific plant needs, avoiding deficiencies and preventing over or under-fertilization, which can harm plants and the environment. Additionally, soil testing determines soil pH levels, enabling adjustments to ensure optimal nutrient availability. Understanding soil texture and structure also improves water retention, drainage, and plant selection. By conducting regular soil tests, you can create a personalized plan that addresses these critical factors, ultimately optimizing your soil's health, supporting thriving plants, and maximizing your food forest's potential.

Performing a soil test is a simple task that becomes easier with practice. Start by choosing a testing method: you can use a home testing kit, available at garden centers, which provides basic information on pH and nutrient levels, or opt for a more detailed analysis by sending your soil sample to a reputable lab, often available through universities or agricultural extensions. When using a home kit, follow the instructions carefully for mixing the soil with solutions and interpreting the results, as different nutrients and pH levels may require varied techniques. For lab testing, adhere to the specific guidelines provided for submitting your sample.

To gather soil samples, use a clean shovel or trowel to collect soil from various areas of your garden at different depths, usually between 4-6 inches, avoiding recently fertilized or composted spots. Combine these samples in a clean container, mix thoroughly to create a composite sample, and let it air dry naturally. Remove any rocks, roots, or debris before testing. After testing, carefully interpret the results, focusing on key indicators like nutrient levels and pH. Labs typically offer specific recommendations for fertilizers based on your soil's needs, and home testing kits may include basic suggestions as well.

Based on your soil test results, take the necessary steps to improve your soil. This could include adding organic matter, adjusting the pH with lime or sulfur, or applying specific nutrient amendments. It's a good idea to keep records of your soil tests and any amendments you make for future reference. I suggest testing your soil in the fall, before commencing cultivation on the food forest, so you can add slow-release nutrients to improve the soil over the winter. Then, test again in the spring to check if the levels are right. If needed, you can make additional adjustments using faster-acting nutrients.

Soil texture, which is determined by the mix of sand, silt, and clay particles, plays a significant role in determining your soil's drainage, water-holding capacity, and nutrient availability. To assess your soil's texture, you'll need to gather a few simple materials, including:

- A transparent glass jar with a lid
  A soil sample (obtained using the previously described method)
- Water
- Dishwashing liquid (optional, to help break down soil particles and aid in the analysis)

Steps to perform a Texture Test
- **Collect a Soil Sample:** Start by gathering soil from different areas of your garden, mixing it together, and removing any debris, just as you would when preparing for a soil test.

- **Prepare the Soil Sample:** Take a small portion of the collected soil and break up any clumps until the soil is loose and crumbly. If the soil is compacted or clumpy, you can add a drop or two of dishwashing liquid to help disperse the particles.
- **Fill the Jar:** Place your soil sample into a jar, filling it about one-third to one-half full.
- **Add Water:** Fill the jar nearly to the top with water, leaving a small space for shaking. If you haven't already added dishwashing liquid, do so now to help break up the soil particles and prevent clumping.
- **Shake Well:** Secure the lid tightly and shake the jar vigorously for several minutes. This process suspends the soil particles in the water, allowing them to separate based on their size and weight.
- **Let it Settle:** After shaking the jar, place it on a flat surface and let it sit undisturbed for at least 24 hours. During this time, the soil particles will settle in layers based on their size and weight. The largest and heaviest particles, sand, will settle at the bottom, followed by the smaller silt particles, and finally, the finest clay particles at the top. You'll notice distinct layers in the jar.
- **Examine the Layers:** To determine the proportion of sand, silt, and clay in your soil, measure the thickness of each layer. Use a ruler or measuring tape to determine the thickness of each layer, and calculate the percentages. For instance, if the sand layer is 1 inch thick and the total soil thickness is 3 inches, sand would make up about 33% of the soil.

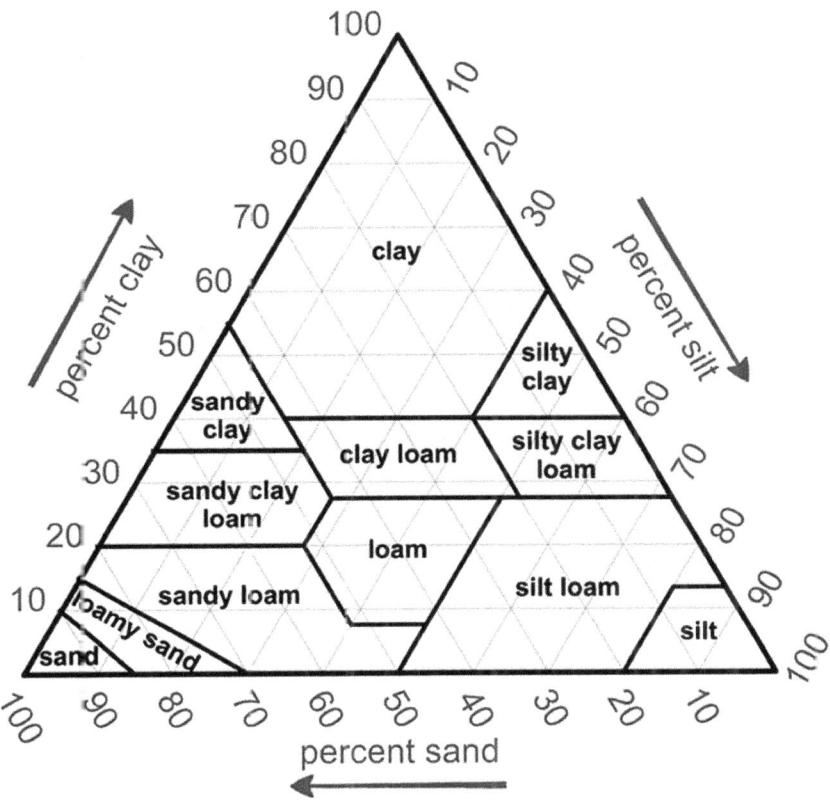

A soil texture triangle

When examining the layers of soil in a jar, you'll typically observe a distinct separation of textures, starting with the thickest bottom layer of sand, which feels gritty to the touch. Above the sand lies the middle layer of silt, a finer and smoother texture that isn't sticky. The topmost layer consists of the finest particles, clay, which has a sticky and smooth feel. Additionally, you may notice organic matter, such as leaves or twigs, floating on the water's surface, further contributing to the soil's composition and structure. This layered separation provides valuable insights into the soil's texture and properties.

Interpreting the result

Understanding your soil's composition is essential for successful gardening, as each soil type has distinct characteristics that influence plant growth. If your soil is composed of over 70% sand, it will drain well but will have difficulty retaining moisture and nutrients due to the solid nature of sand particles. This results in dry, low-fertility soil that requires more frequent watering and feeding, making it challenging for most plants to thrive. In contrast, soil with a high silt content (over 70%) offers good drainage and moderate water retention. Silty soil is nutrient-rich and holds moisture well, but too much silt can limit oxygen availability to plant roots, causing them to wilt even when water is present.

Clay soil, with over 70% clay content, retains water excessively and drains poorly due to limited airflow between the tightly packed particles. When dry, clay soil becomes hard and compacted, making it difficult to work with. Although rich in nutrients, the dense structure can prevent plant roots from accessing the necessary nutrients and oxygen. Loam, which has a balanced mixture of sand, silt, and clay (about 40-40-20%), is the optimal soil texture.. Loam combines the best qualities of each component: sand promotes drainage and air flow, silt helps with moisture retention, and clay adds nutrients while balancing moisture levels. Loamy soil is optimal for gardening, providing a healthy environment for plant growth.

To improve your soil's texture based on its composition:

- Add organic matter, such as compost, to clay soils to enhance drainage and aeration. Planting cover crops between gardening seasons can also help maintain these qualities.
- In sandy soils, incorporating compost or well-rotted manure will enhance water retention. Cover crops can stabilize the soil and increase organic content.
- For loamy soils, maintaining their structure involves regularly adding organic matter to replenish nutrients and support healthy microbial activity.

No matter the soil type, consistently adding organic matter is key to improving or maintaining soil quality. Remember, soil testing should be done periodically to ensure your soil remains in the best condition for healthy plants and abundant harvests.

Strategies for improving soil structure and increasing organic matter on your food forest

Improving soil structure and increasing organic matter are essential for cultivating a thriving food forest, as these two aspects are closely interconnected. Soil structure refers to the arrangement of soil particles into aggregates, which plays a crucial role in water infiltration, aeration, and root growth. Organic matter, composed of living and dead organisms in the soil, enhances soil structure by binding particles together, improving water retention, and supplying nutrients for plant growth.

To build soil structure, it's important to minimize disturbance through practices like no-till or minimal tillage, which help preserve existing aggregates and promote the growth of beneficial organisms. Planting cover crops also plays a significant role in protecting the soil from erosion, adding organic matter, and improving soil structure through their root systems. A diverse range of plants with varying root depths creates a complex network of root channels, further enhancing soil structure. Additionally, incorporating compost and manure into the soil provides essential nutrients and humus, which bind soil particles together, contributing to a stable and fertile structure.

Increasing organic matter in the soil involves several practices that work in tandem with those that build soil structure. Applying a thick layer of organic mulch helps protect the soil, suppress weeds, and add organic matter as it decomposes. Composting kitchen scraps, yard waste, and other organic materials enriches the soil, while the continued use of cover crops adds further organic content. If applicable, integrating animals like chickens or ducks into the food forest can provide manure, which is rich in organic matter and beneficial for soil health. Leaving crop residues on the soil surface to decompose naturally also contributes to the organic matter, further improving soil quality

Regular soil testing is vital to assess its organic matter content and structure, allowing for timely adjustments to ensure optimal soil health. Building healthy soil is a gradual process that requires patience and consistent application of these practices. By observing the condition of the soil and making necessary adjustments, you can effectively manage and enhance soil structure and organic matter content. Additionally, considering the use of biochar, a charcoal-like substance, can further improve soil structure and water retention, providing long-term benefits to your food forest.

REDUCING WASTE USING A CLOSED LOOP SYSTEM

A food forest flourishes by embracing a closed-loop system that minimizes waste and maximizes resource efficiency, where every element is interconnected and valuable resources are continually cycled back into the ecosystem. This is achieved through a harmonious combination of nutrient cycling strategies: composting converts food scraps, plant matter, and animal manure into nutrient-rich compost, while cover crops like nitrogen-fixing legumes add organic matter and prevent soil erosion, and mulching recycles leaves, grass clippings, and other organic materials to retain moisture, suppress weeds, and further enrich the soil, creating a thriving and regenerative food forest ecosystem.

Effective water management is important in a food forest, and can be achieved through a combination of strategies that work together to maximize water efficiency. You can lessen your need for outside water sources by using rainwater harvesting to capture and store rainfall. Additionally, creating contour ditches known as swales helps to capture and slowly release rainwater, improving soil moisture and reducing runoff. Finally, selecting plants that are adapted to your region's climate and water availability, also known as water-wise plant selection, ensures that your food forest is resilient and thriving, even in times of drought or water scarcity, ultimately creating a sustainable and regenerative water management system.

Dispersed energy efficiency strategies can be integrated to create a cohesive approach to reducing energy consumption in a food forest. By harnessing solar power to generate electricity for essential systems like pumps, tools, and lighting, you can significantly decrease reliance on non-renewable energy sources. You should also prioritize manual labor for tasks like pruning, planting, and harvesting not only to reduce energy consumption but also fosters a deeper connection with the land. Furthermore, selecting efficient equipment and tools designed for low energy consumption optimizes energy use, creating a harmonious balance between technology and manual labor, ultimately leading to a more sustainable and energy-efficient food forest ecosystem.

A comprehensive waste reduction strategy in a food forest should involve a multi-faceted approach that minimizes waste and maximizes efficiency by preserving surplus produce through canning, drying, or fermentation, propagating plants from cuttings, seeds, or divisions to reduce the need for new plant purchases, and integrating closed-loop animal systems where animals like chickens or goats consume food scraps and produce manure, thereby creating a cyclical system where waste is transformed into valuable resources, reducing the need for external inputs and promoting a regenerative and sustainable food forest ecosystem.

A flourishing food forest ecosystem requires integrating multiple components that work together to create a regenerative and sustainable environment. This is accomplished by designing a site-specific system tailored to local climate, soil conditions, and available resources, and incorporating ecosystem services such as pollinator habitats to support beneficial insects, wildlife habitats to provide food and shelter, and carbon sequestration through organic matter to increase soil carbon storage. Additionally, continuous observation and adaptation ensure the system s resilience, while promoting diversity in plants and animals fosters a balanced and thriving ecosystem, ultimately creating a harmonious and productive food forest that benefits both people and the environment.

IMPLEMENTING A CLIMATE RESILIENT FOOD FOREST

Climate is a critical factor in the success of a food forest, and understanding its various components is essential for creating a thriving ecosystem. Key climate factors to consider include temperature-related elements such as frost dates, which determine the planting schedule and selection of species that can tolerate the earliest and latest frosts; heat tolerance, which involves choosing plants that can withstand high temperatures during hot summers; and cold hardiness, which requires selecting species that can survive winter temperatures without damage, ultimately ensuring that your food forest is resilient and productive throughout the year.

Precipitation patterns, which includes annual rainfall distribution and seasonal variations, which informs the selection of drought-tolerant plants that can withstand periods of water scarcity, and the implementation of water harvesting systems to capture and store rainwater, thereby creating a resilient and sustainable ecosystem that maximizes the use of this precious resource. A food forest's design must also consider the interconnected factors of sunlight and wind patterns to create a harmonious and thriving ecosystem. This involves determining the site's sun exposure throughout the year, selecting plants with suitable shade tolerance, and strategically placing them to optimize sunlight reception. Assessing prevailing wind patterns informs the protection of vulnerable plants and the creation of natural or artificial windbreaks to mitigate wind impact, ultimately ensuring that the food forest is resilient and productive in the face of varying environmental conditions.

Adapting to extreme weather events and climate change is essential for a food forest's long-term success, and this can be achieved by considering multiple factors. By selecting plants and preparing the site to mitigate flood damage, implementing water-saving strategies and choosing drought-tolerant species for droughts, and protecting plants from strong winds and heavy rainfall during storms, you can create a resilient ecosystem. Researching future climate projections for your region, increasing plant diversity to adapt to changing conditions, and focusing on building resilience through soil health, water management, and biodiversity will help your food forest bloom in the face of uncertainty, ensuring a sustainable and regenerative environment for years to come. So now let's explore some examples plants based on different climate zones where they flourish:

Temperate Climate

- **Characterized by:** Distinct seasons with warm summers and cold winters.

- **Example Plants:**
  - Trees: Apple, pear, plum, cherry, walnut, hazelnut
  - Shrubs: Raspberry, blackberry, currant, elderberry
  - Herbs: Mint, thyme, rosemary, sage
  - Groundcovers: Strawberries, creeping thyme, clover

Mediterranean Climate

- **Characterized by:** Hot, dry summers and mild, rainy winters.
- **Example Plants:**
  - Trees: Olive, fig, almond, pomegranate
  - Shrubs: Rosemary, lavender, juniper
  - Herbs: Oregano, thyme, sage
  - Groundcovers: Creeping thyme, rosemary

Arid Climate

- **Characterized by:** Low rainfall and high temperatures.
- **Example Plants:**
  - Trees: Date palm, olive, pomegranate
  - Shrubs: Juniper, sagebrush
  - Herbs: Rosemary, thyme
  - Groundcovers: Creeping thyme, succulents

This is just a general overview. It's essential to research specific plant varieties suitable for your location.

DESIGN PRINCIPLES OF A FOOD FOREST

Designing a food forest involves creating a system that mimics the structure and function of a natural forest while producing an abundance of edible plants. This approach relies on key design principles that ensure the system is sustainable, efficient, diverse, and beneficial for both the environment and human well-being.

One of the foundational principles is mimicking nature. This includes using polyculture, where a variety of plants are grown together, similar to a natural ecosystem. Additionally, the concept of guilding involves grouping plants that benefit each other, such as pairing nitrogen-fixing plants with fruit trees. Understanding natural plant succession is also crucial, as it guides the development of the food forest, ensuring that plants are introduced in a sequence that mirrors natural processes.

Efficiency and sustainability are achieved by prioritizing perennial plants, which return year after year, reducing the need for replanting while increasing overall yield. Closed-loop systems are implemented to recycle nutrients and water within the food forest, minimizing the need for external inputs. Soil building is another critical aspect, focusing on improving soil health through composting, cover crops, and minimal disturbance, which in turn supports long-term productivity.

The principle of diversity and resilience is addressed by creating multiple layers within the food forest, with plants at different heights such as canopy, understory, shrubs, herbs, and ground cover. This stratification creates a diverse ecosystem that is more resilient to pests and environmental changes. The concept of edge effects is also utilized, maximizing productivity by taking advantage of the areas where different plant communities meet. Biodiversity is encouraged throughout the system, promoting a balance of plant and animal life that aids in natural pest control and overall ecosystem health.

Incorporating human well-being into the design ensures that the food forest provides more than just environmental benefits. It offers food security by providing a sustainable and reliable source of food. The food forest also supports wildlife and pollinators, creating habitats that enhance biodiversity. Additionally, it serves as a space for education and recreation, offering opportunities for learning and enjoyment.

Finally, site-specific design is crucial for the success of a food forest. The design must be tailored to the local climate, soil, and available space to ensure that the system thrives. Efficient water management techniques, such as water harvesting and retention, are implemented to conserve resources. Energy efficiency is also prioritized, with careful planning and design aimed at minimizing energy inputs. By integrating these principles, a food forest can be designed to function as a self-sustaining, productive ecosystem that benefits both the environment and the people who interact with it.

DESIGN PATTERNS

While there's no one-size-fits-all pattern, several general design approaches can be adopted:

The guilding pattern: Guilding is a core permaculture design principle that involves grouping plants together based on their symbiotic relationships and complementary needs. It mimics the natural patterns found in forests, where different species interact to create a self-sustaining ecosystem.

Guild Dynamics

- **Nitrogen-fixing plants:** These plants convert atmospheric nitrogen into a form usable by other plants. Examples include legumes like beans, peas, and clover.
- **Cover crops:** Protect soil, prevent erosion, and add organic matter. They can also suppress weeds. Examples include oats, rye, and buckwheat.
- **Companion plants:** Enhance the growth of other plants through beneficial interactions. For instance, basil repels insects from tomatoes.
- **Support plants:** Provide structural support for other plants, like climbing beans on a trellis.

In a nitrogen-fixing guild, a harmonious combination of plants work together to create a mutually beneficial ecosystem, consisting of components like alfalfa, clover, peas, and fruit trees such as apple and plum. In this guild, alfalfa and clover enrich the soil with nitrogen through their nitrogen-fixing properties, benefiting the fruit trees, while the fruit trees provide shade for the legumes, which prefer cooler conditions, creating a symbiotic relationship that enhances soil fertility and promotes healthy growth for all members of the guild.

The shade-tolerant guild, comprising ferns, hostas, and woodland strawberries, showcases how ferns and hostas create a weed-suppressing, moisture-retaining ground cover, while strawberries produce edible fruit, demonstrating a harmonious relationship. Similarly, the herb garden guild, consisting of basil, oregano, rosemary, tomatoes, and marigolds, highlights how basil and marigolds repel insects, while oregano and rosemary enhance the flavor of tomatoes, exemplifying the benefits of thoughtfully combining plants to create a thriving and productive ecosystem.

Another example is the forest garden guild which is a thoughtfully designed plant community that leverages the unique characteristics of each species to create a thriving ecosystem, as exemplified by the combination of a walnut tree, hazelnuts, garlic, ramps, and violets. In this guild, the walnut tree's allelopathic properties suppress the growth of other plants, creating space for understory plants like hazelnuts to flourish, while garlic and ramps, which are shade-tolerant, provide early-season harvests, and violets contribute to the diversity and resilience of the ecosystem, demonstrating how intentional plant pairing can foster a productive and balanced relationship among species.

Some case studies of successful guilds demonstrate the power of intentional plant pairing, as seen in The Star Nursery Guild, popularized by Sepp Holzer, which combines fruit trees, berries, and nitrogen-fixing plants like alfalfa and clover to create a diverse and self-sustaining ecosystem with minimal input. Similarly, The Three Sisters Guild, a traditional Native American combination of corn, beans, and squash, showcases a synergistic relationship where corn provides structural support for beans, beans add nitrogen to the soil, and squash covers the ground, suppressing weeds and retaining moisture, exemplifying how guilds can foster resilient and productive ecosystems through mutually beneficial relationships among plants.

When designing a guild, it's essential to consider several key factors to create a resilient ecosystem. This involves selecting plants that are well-suited to your local climate and soil conditions, ensuring adequate spacing and compatibility among plants to prevent competition for resources, planning for the long-term development of the guild and the role of each plant in its succession, and prioritizing diversity by incorporating a variety of plant species to increase ecosystem services and resilience, ultimately creating a harmonious and balanced plant community that functions optimally over time.

DESIGN DIVERSITY AND EDGE EFFECT

Designing a diverse and productive food forest requires a careful arrangement of plant species, each fulfilling specific roles to support a resilient, self-sustaining ecosystem. This holistic approach leverages diversity principles and the benefits of edge effects, integrating multiple ecological functions and microclimates. A fundamental strategy in food forest design is layering and arranging plants into a vertical structure to maximize space, light capture, and soil health. Layers range from towering canopy trees, like walnuts or apples, to smaller understory trees, which thrive under partial shade, providing habitat and enriching the soil with leaf drop. The forest floor is populated by a dense herbaceous layer of ground covers—like mint, comfrey, and thyme—protecting soil, shading roots, and attracting pollinators. Deep-rooted plants occupy the root layer, enhancing soil structure, while vines and climbers utilize vertical space, producing food with minimal footprint. This layering approach optimizes productivity and prevents erosion while mimicking a natural forest ecosystem.

A Food Forest Transition zone

Functional diversity is equally crucial, with each plant playing a distinct ecological role. Nitrogen-fixers such as clover and black locust add essential nutrients, supporting nearby plants. Nutrient accumulators like yarrow and comfrey draw minerals from deep soil layers, making them accessible to shallow-rooted plants. Pollinator plants such as lavender and echinacea sustain essential pollinators, boosting fruit yields, while aromatic pest-repellent plants like garlic and rosemary deter pests naturally. This diversity of functions fosters resilience and a balanced ecosystem, allowing the forest to thrive even if one species struggles. A food forest also evolves with seasonal and successional diversity, ensuring productivity and adaptability over time. Seasonal planting provides year-round harvest and habitat, with early bloomers like strawberries complementing late-season apples. The forest matures through successional planting—starting with fast-growing pioneers, such as nitrogen-fixing species, which prepare the soil for longer-lived trees. As these pioneers eventually phase out, mature canopy trees take their place, creating a dynamic, self-renewing system. Incorporating genetic diversity within species, such as planting multiple apple cultivars, helps the forest adapt to changing conditions and reduces vulnerability to pests and disease outbreaks. This variety in genetics strengthens the system's stability and sustainability.

Edge effects maximize productivity by creating transition zones between ecosystems. These edges, where different habitats meet, support a wide range of species and microclimates, enhancing biodiversity and yields. For example, placing shrubs and berry bushes at the forest's edge utilizes partial shade and full sun, while ponds create moist microclimates that support both terrestrial and aquatic life. Curving paths and borders increase the edge surface, fostering these rich interfaces. Edge zones, the borders between different habitats, are particularly valuable for increasing biodiversity, productivity, and specialized growing environments. These edges, where varying conditions overlap, host a high density of species due to fluctuating resources, creating warmer, cooler, wetter, or drier microclimates to support diverse plant needs. For example, a sunny area meeting a shaded grove offers conditions for partial-sun plants that wouldn't thrive in full sun or shade alone. This natural variety boosts overall productivity, with edge areas often yielding more food per area than interior spaces of single-purpose plantings. To enhance these edge effects, forest borders should be designed to maximize interaction between habitats. Curved or meandering borders, rather than straight ones, create more edge space, fostering biodiversity. Transition zones—such as berry bushes planted where open sunlight meets the tree canopy—allow species to benefit from both light and shade. Adding water features, like ponds or streams, introduces moisture-rich microclimates along the water's edge, encouraging aquatic and terrestrial life. Meanwhile, windbreaks or dense vegetation at edges reduce soil moisture loss and shield inner forest plants, creating a favorable environment for both wind-tolerant and wind-sensitive species.

Example of edge effect is a Shade grown coffee thriving under forest canopy

When implementing these diversity and edge principles, a thoughtful approach to layout, species selection, and site management is crucial. Site analysis, considering sunlight, soil, and water flow, helps identify areas ideal for edge effects and microclimates. Zoning and design decisions should reflect these conditions, with pathways, ponds, or field edges strategically placed to maximize productive borders. Species should be chosen to fit microclimates and edge zones, with each plant fulfilling a unique function—whether for nitrogen fixation, pest deterrence, or pollinator support. Regular observation and adaptation, such as removing pioneer plants to allow mature trees space, keep the system balanced and responsive to growth patterns. By integrating layered diversity and designing with edge effects in mind, a food forest becomes a regenerative ecosystem. With minimal maintenance, it remains productive, resilient to pests and weather changes, and ecologically balanced, providing food, habitat, and soil enrichment naturally.

Lush vegetation arising from the edge where water meet soil

CHAPTER FOUR

PLANT SELECTION AND CARE

Choosing the best plants and caring for them in a food forest is essential to fostering a self-sustaining, resilient ecosystem that produces food, provides habitat, and regenerates soil health. Let's explore a step-by-step approach to optimal plant selection and care strategies for a thriving food forest.

Understanding Site Conditions

Before selecting plants, thoroughly analyze your site to understand the existing soil, water, sunlight, and microclimate conditions. To ensure each plant grows well in a food forest, it's essential to understand specific site conditions, which guide optimal plant placement and reduce maintenance needs. Start by testing your soil's pH, structure, drainage, and nutrient levels. Food forests generally perform best in slightly acidic to neutral soils with good drainage. For low-quality soil, prioritize plants like nitrogen-fixers and nutrient accumulators to enhance soil health in the early stages. Next, evaluate water availability by observing natural water flow and retention areas. Moisture-loving plants should go in zones where water pools or is retained, while drought-resistant plants are better suited to drier spots. Finally, track sunlight patterns throughout the day. Place sun-loving plants in areas with full exposure, and reserve partially shaded zones for understory species that require less light. By matching each plant's needs to its location, you increase survival rates, reduce care requirements, and help create a thriving, resilient ecosystem.

Choosing Plants for Functional Roles

A productive food forest relies on plant species that each play specific ecological roles, supporting a self-sustaining ecosystem. Large canopy trees like apples, pears, walnuts, and chestnuts create the forest structure, providing food, shade, and organic matter through leaf drop. To enrich soil fertility naturally, nitrogen-fixers like black locust, alders, and clovers are distributed across the forest, adding essential nutrients that benefit neighboring plants. Nutrient accumulators like comfrey, dandelion, and yarrow bring minerals up from the subsoil, enriching the topsoil and benefiting the entire plant community. Biodiversity is further strengthened by pollinator attractors such as lavender, bee balm, and echinacea, which draw pollinators necessary for fruit and seed production. Pest-repellent plants like garlic, marigold, and rosemary provide natural pest control, shielding vulnerable plants and reducing the need for chemical inputs. Ground covers like clover, creeping thyme, and strawberries also play a vital role, protecting soil from erosion, retaining moisture, and suppressing weeds. By choosing plants based on these essential roles, each element of the food forest works in harmony to support the others, minimizing external inputs and fostering a robust ecosystem.

Prioritizing Genetic and Species Diversity

Diversity is crucial for establishing a food forest, requiring a variety of species and genetic variations within those species. This diversity enhances disease and pest resistance, as different varieties have unique vulnerabilities, thereby minimizing the risk of widespread issues affecting the entire plant population. It also promotes adaptation to microclimates, allowing for the selection of cultivars that thrive in specific site conditions, such as cold-tolerant apples in shaded areas or heat-resistant varieties in sunny spots. Furthermore, incorporating a range

Emphasizing Plant Compatibility and Companion Planting

Certain plant combinations within a food forest, known as companion planting, can significantly enhance growth, improve soil health, and deter pests. For example, the Three Sisters, a classic combination of corn, beans, and squash demonstrates this principle, as corn provides support for climbing beans, beans fix nitrogen in the soil, and squash serves as ground cover to suppress weeds. Moreso, planting garlic around apple trees helps repel pests like aphids, thereby boosting the trees' overall health. Another beneficial pairing is nasturtium with brassicas, where nasturtiums deter cabbage worms and other pests that commonly affect crops like kale, broccoli, and cabbage. By prioritizing combinations that offer mutual benefits—such as nutrient cycling, pest deterrence, and shade—you can create a more robust and productive ecosystem within your food forest.

Planning for Succession

Food forests undergo natural evolution, making it essential to consider plant selection for each stage of development. **Pioneer species**, such as nitrogen-fixing alders and hardy elderberries, are fast-growing and help improve soil quality while creating microclimates for slower-growing plants. As the forest matures, **mid-succession species**, including productive fruit trees and shrubs, are introduced to enhance biodiversity and food production. Ultimately, **climax species**, such as large canopy trees like walnuts and chestnuts, along with durable perennials, establish the mature food forest. This thoughtful planning for succession ensures that as soil and shade conditions change over time, each stage of plants supports the next, fostering a self-sustaining ecosystem.

Caring for a Food Forest

While food forests generally require less intensive maintenance than traditional gardens, several critical care practices are essential for establishing and maintaining a healthy ecosystem. Mulching and Groundcovers play a vital role by retaining moisture, regulating soil temperature, and suppressing weeds. Using organic materials like straw, leaves, or wood chips not only provides these benefits but also enriches soil health as the mulch breaks down over time. Additionally, ground covers like clover and thyme act as living mulches, reducing erosion and offering habitat for beneficial organisms. Watering Strategy is crucial, particularly in the first few years when young plants need consistent hydration to develop strong roots. Implementing swales—shallow trenches that capture rainwater—can facilitate passive irrigation. Once established, the food forest often relies on natural rainfall for moisture. Pruning and Thinning are necessary to promote plant health by enhancing airflow and sunlight penetration. Thinning out crowded areas, especially during the early stages, prevents competition and encourages the growth of dominant species. As the forest matures, some pioneer species may need to be removed to allow space for mature canopy trees. Managing Pests Naturally involves encouraging natural predators by creating habitat diversity that attracts birds, ladybugs, and other beneficial insects. Strategically using pest-repellent plants and implementing companion planting can further reduce pest issues. If necessary, organic pest control methods such as neem oil or insecticidal soap can be applied to manage outbreaks. Lastly,

Monitoring and Observing the forest is key to adapting care practices. Regularly assessing plant health, growth patterns, and species interactions allows for adjustments in the forest layout or plant selection based on observed conditions, such as identifying areas that retain more water and might be better suited for moisture-loving plants. This ongoing observation helps the forest evolve harmoniously with changing conditions, ensuring its long-term resilience and productivity.

Gradually Introducing New Species

Once your forest is established, consider introducing new species gradually to fill gaps or diversify the ecosystem. Perennials, herbs, and small shrubs are often easier to integrate without disturbing established plants. This practice maintains a dynamic, adaptive environment, allowing your food forest to support diverse species without intensive intervention.

CHOOSING THE RIGHT PLANTS

Canopy cover

Apple tree.

Pear tree

Chestnuts.

Walnuts

Oak.

Pecan

Almonds.

Mulberry

SUB-CANOPY LAYER (Smaller Trees)

Peach

Figs

SHRUB LAYER

Blueberry

Raspberry

HERBACEOUS LAYER (Perennials and Annuals)

Rhubarb Plant.

Asparagus

Borage

Parsley

GROUND COVER LAYER

Strawberry

Clover

Oregano

Creeping Thyme

ROOT LAYER

Garlic

Jerusalem Artichoke

Sweet Potato

Ginger

VERTICAL LAYER (Climbers and Vines)

Grapes

Kiwi vines

Passion fruit

Climbing Beans

NITROGEN FIXING PLANTS

CANOPY LAYER

Black Locust

Alder Tree

Honey Locust

73

SHRUB LAYER

Siberian Pea Shrub

Autumn Olive

Sea Buckthorn

GROUND COVER AND HERB LAYER

Lupine

Vetch

VINE LAYER

Scarlet runner beans

Peas

PLANT GUILDS AND COMPANION PLANTING

In a food forest, plant guilds and companion planting strategies work together to create a self-sustaining ecosystem that maximizes productivity, supports soil health, attracts pollinators, and reduces pests. Each plant guild combines specific plants that serve complementary roles, enhancing the resilence and diversity of the ecosystem.

For example, an Apple Tree Guild includes apple trees surrounded by nitrogen-fixers like clover and comfrey to boost soil fertility, pollinator-attracting plants such as bee balm and lavender, pest-repellent plants like garlic and chives, and ground covers like thyme to retain moisture and suppress weeds. Similarly, the Three Sisters Guild features corn, beans, and squash, where corn provides a trellis for beans, beans enrich the soil with nitrogen, and squash covers the ground to conserve moisture and reduce weeds.

A Nut Tree Guild may include chestnut, walnut, or hazelnut trees with nitrogen-fixing shrubs like Siberian pea and pollinator-attracting flowers like yarrow. Comfrey acts as a dynamic accumulator, drawing minerals up from the soil, while ground covers like strawberry help retain moisture. Likewise, a Cherry Tree Guild combines cherry trees with nitrogen-fixers like goumi, pollinator-friendly plants like echinacea, pest-repelling garlic, and ground covers like mint to create a thriving undergrowth.

The Berry Bush Guild includes shrubs like blueberries and raspberries with nitrogen-fixers such as clover, dynamic accumulators like comfrey, pollinator attractors such as marigolds, and pest-repelling plants like tansy. Low-growing herbs like thyme as ground cover support moisture conservation. Additionally, an Herbal Guild of lavender, rosemary, yarrow, and fennel aids pest control, with herbs repelling unwanted insects while yarrow and lavender draw in pollinators essential for fruiting.

Together, these guilds and companion plantings provide key benefits: nitrogen-fixers and deep-rooted plants enhance soil health, pest-repellent plants provide natural pest control, pollinator-attracting flowers improve yields, and groundcovers ensure efficient space use. This integrated approach creates a resilient, diverse food forest that supports itself naturally.

THE BEST COMPANION PLANT COMBINATION

Companion planting is the practice of pairing plants that benefit each other in various ways, including pest control, nutrient sharing, soil improvement, or enhanced growth. In a food forest, where plants are integrated in multi-layered systems, companion planting can help create a balanced and resilient ecosystem. The Three Sisters—corn, beans, and squash—are a classic Native American combination that works best in sunny areas with ample warmth and space; corn provides a natural trellis for beans to climb, beans fix nitrogen in the soil to benefit corn and squash, and squash spreads across the ground, acting as a living mulch that suppresses weeds and retains soil moisture. Tomatoes benefit from basil, which repels insects like aphids, whiteflies, and mosquitoes and may even enhance tomato flavor, while marigolds help repel pests like nematodes and whiteflies that can affect tomato roots and leaves; planting basil and marigold near tomatoes creates a healthier environment, reducing disease risk and increasing flavor.

Carrots grow deep in the soil while onions and garlic grow shallowy, minimizing competition for nutrients; onions and garlic release sulfur compounds that repel carrot flies, aphids, and other pests, so this combination maximizes soil use while helping protect carrots naturally from pests. The cabbage family (brassicas) benefits from aromatic herbs like rosemary, sage, and dill that repel pests such as cabbage worms and aphids and attract beneficial insects like ladybugs and lacewings; placing these herbs around brassicas creates a natural pest barrier that enhances growth. Radishes can be grown close to cucumbers to deter cucumber beetles, and radish leaves act as a decoy for flea beetles that might otherwise target cucumbers; planting radishes as a trap crop helps protect cucumbers while also providing a quick-growing vegetable crop. The apple tree guild, with apple trees paired with chives, comfrey, and clover, supports healthy growth, pest control, and soil fertility; chives and garlic repel pests such as aphids and mites, comfrey's deep roots bring up nutrients that enrich the soil as living mulch, and clover fixes nitrogen, enriching the soil for the apple tree.

Roses benefit from garlic planted around them, which helps repel aphids, black spot, and Japanese beetles; garlic's sulfur also reduces mildew on roses, promoting healthier blooms, making this pairing a beautiful and practical choice for food forests with ornamental plants or integrated garden areas. Peppers benefit from carrots, which aerate the soil as they grow deep, while carrots are undisturbed by the shallow-rooted peppers, creating a harmonious combination that optimizes space, especially in small food forests, and minimizes nutrient competition. Grapes benefit from hyssop, which repels pests like flea beetles that can harm grape vines and also attracts bees, enhancing pollination for nearby flowering plants; this pairing is effective in vineyards or trellised sections of food forests where grapes grow vertically. Spinach grows well in the shade of strawberry plants, which provide ground cover that conserves moisture and keeps the soil cool for spinach; this combination makes efficient use of space and creates a mutually beneficial microenvironment. Horseradish planted near potatoes repels pests like potato beetles and aphids, while its deep roots also help aerate the soil; placing horseradish around the perimeter of potato patches provides natural pest protection. Nasturtium, grown around fruit trees, attracts aphids as a trap crop away from the fruit trees and also attracts pollinators and beneficial insects like predatory wasps, helping deter pests and boosting fruit yield.

Sunflowers provide shade and support for cucumbers to climb, protecting them from sun scald on hot days; this combination works well for vertical space in a food forest and is visually appealing. Beans and beets grow well together, as beans fix nitrogen in the soil that benefits nutrient-demanding beets, and both crops coexist without competing heavily for space or nutrients; this pairing improves soil fertility and is ideal for planting in rows or raised beds. Lettuce and carrots can be grown in the shade of radishes, which grow quickly and provide some shade, while radishes deter pests and help break up compacted soil, benefiting lettuce and carrots; growing these together creates a diverse, layered planting that maximizes space and deters pests.

Companion planting offers multiple benefits in a food forest, including pest control as some plants act as natural repellents, trap crops, or attract beneficial insects that keep pest populations down; nutrient cycling, where nitrogen-fixing plants like beans and clover enrich the soil for nutrient-demanding crops; enhanced growth and yield, as companion plants improve each other's growth rates, health, and flavor; soil health and moisture retention through ground covers like clover and squash, which suppress weeds, retain moisture, and prevent erosion; and increased biodiversity by promoting a variety of plants and habitats, creating a resilient and balanced ecosystem. In a food forest, companion planting enhances productivity, builds soil health, and supports a self-sustaining, low-maintenance environment, contributing to the overall success and resilience of the system.

CHAPTER FIVE

PROPAGATION AND PLANTING

Propagation and planting are essential processes in establishing a food forest, creating a diverse, resilient, and self-sustaining ecosystem. Propagation, the method of reproducing plants from seeds or plant parts like cuttings, grafts, and roots, enables the growth of varied plant species that fulfill specific ecological roles. Planting, which involves establishing these propagated plants in ways that mimic natural forest structures, creates interactive layers that promote symbiosis. Together, propagation and planting establish a food forest that provides food, conserves resources, and supports wildlife by imitating the resilience of a natural forest.

Propagation techniques in a food forest aim to cultivate a range of plants, each performing roles that enhance ecosystem balance. These techniques include starting plants from seeds, taking cuttings, layering, division, and grafting Seeds are chosen based on local conditions to promote biodiversity, allowing trees, shrubs, herbs, and ground covers to develop root systems well-suited to the forest environment. Cuttings, which use parts of a plant like stems or leaves to grow a clone of the parent, are ideal for propagating perennials such as berry bushes, preserving desirable traits. Layering involves bending a branch to the ground and covering it with soil to promote root formation, a low-effort way to propagate fruit trees and shrubs. Division works well for certain herbs and ground covers, allowing plants like rhubarb and strawberries to be separated into parts that quickly establish in the soil. Grafting, a method commonly used for fruit trees, joins plant parts to create unique varieties that share a root system, enhancing biodiversity in the canopy layer.

Planting in a food forest requires careful planning to arrange plants in layers and guilds, allowing beneficial interactions as in a natural forest. By arranging plants in layers—such as canopy trees, understory shrubs, herbaceous plants, ground covers, root vegetables, and vines—a food forest maximizes biodiversity, reduces competition for sunlight, and ensures efficient sharing of resources. Plant guilds combine plants that work together, often including nitrogen-fixing species for soil fertility, flowers that attract pollinators, and ground covers that suppress weeds. Succession planting, where fast-growing plants improve the soil for slower-growing trees, allows the forest to adapt over time. This process creates a dynamic environment where species composition shifts naturally as the forest matures, maintaining balance in response to changing conditions.

Preparing the site for planting often involves enriching the soil with compost or mulch, which retains moisture and suppresses weeds while enhancing soil health as it breaks down. Proper spacing is essential to allow for plant maturity, especially for trees that need sufficient light and airflow, while smaller plants can grow more densely to mimic the diversity of natural forests. Selecting locations that provide the right sun exposure and moisture for each plant ensures they thrive; for example, canopy trees create partial shade that benefits shade-loving ground covers and understory plants. Mulch is added around planting areas to retain moisture, prevent erosion, and regulate soil temperature, while ground covers like clover or thyme serve as living mulches that improve soil health.

Propagation and planting contribute to biodiversity, low maintenance, sustainable food production, and soil and water conservation in food forests. High biodiversity strengthens resilience against pests, diseases, and climate variations. Once established, food forests require minimal inputs as nitrogen-fixing plants enrich the soil, ground covers reduce weed growth, and natural plant communities lessen the need for irrigation and pest control. Food forests provide a sustainable yield of fruits, nuts, vegetables, herbs, and medicinal plants through multi-layered planting that maximizes productivity. Additionally, dense root systems stabilize soil, prevent erosion, and conserve water, with ground covers and mulch helping to retain moisture.

While propagation and planting lay the foundation for a food forest, long-term care is essential as the ecosystem evolves. Plants may need pruning harvesting, or replacement to maintain balance, and as the forest matures, certain species may dominate or decline, requiring adjustments to preserve diversity and productivity. By carefully selecting propagation methods and employing strategic planting, a food forest develops into a self-sustaining ecosystem that benefits both people and the planet, providing food and fostering biodiversity within a sustainable framework that mirrors natural resilience.

SEED STARTING

Starting seeds in a food forest is an essential process that lays the foundation for a diverse and resilient ecosystem. Unlike traditional gardens, where plants are often started in controlled environments and transplanted, food forest seed starting combines both traditional and natural methods. This approach creates layers of plants that mimic natural forests and form productive, low-maintenance landscapes. Here's a comprehensive look at the considerations and steps involved in seed starting within a food forest setting.

1. Choosing the Right Seeds

The first step in starting seeds for a food forest is selecting plants that will not only thrive in the local climate and soil but also serve multiple roles in the ecosystem. Key types of plants include:

- Canopy Plants: Tall trees, like fruit and nut trees, form the forest's highest layer and should be chosen based on the site's climate and soil. For example, apples, chestnuts, and walnuts are common choices for temperate food forests.
- Nitrogen Fixers: These plants enrich the soil by adding nitrogen, an essential nutrient for plant growth. Clover, peas, and lupine are effective nitrogen-fixers that support the soil health of neighboring plants.
- Dynamic Accumulators: Plants like comfrey and yarrow have deep roots that pull minerals from the subsoil, helping enrich the surface soil as their leaves decompose.
- Ground Covers: Low-growing plants such as strawberries and thyme cover bare soil, conserve moisture, and suppress weeds.
- Pollinator Plants: Flowers and herbs, such as bee balm, lavender, and echinacea, attract pollinators and beneficial insects that improve yields and help control pests.

Starting with seeds instead of mature plants allows for greater biodiversity. You can experiment with species and varieties that naturally adapt to the ecosystem, which enhances resilience.

2. Timing and Season Considerations

Seed starting in a food forest is generally divided into two phases:

- Spring Planting: Spring is ideal for starting most annuals, perennials, and biennials. Warmer soil and longer daylight hours support germination and growth, making it a suitable time for vegetables, herbs, and most fruiting plants.
- Fall Planting: Certain plants, especially those that benefit from a period of cold stratification (like some fruit and nut trees), are best planted in the fall. Cold stratification mimics the natural process of overwintering seeds, helping them to germinate in spring.

In a food forest, succession planting is also essential. This approach involves planting crops at different times or in overlapping cycles, ensuring that as one plant matures and dies, another takes its place. This cycle maintains soil cover and productivity throughout the year.

3. Site Preparation and Soil Enhancement

Preparing the site is crucial before starting seeds. In a food forest, you'll often need to prepare multiple microenvironments to support the needs of different plants:

- Soil Building: Start by enhancing soil health through compost, mulch, and, if needed, amendments based on soil tests. Adding compost and organic matter ensures that young plants will have access to nutrients as they grow.

- Creating Microclimates: Food forests are layered, with taller trees shading smaller plants and protecting tender seedlings from direct sun and wind. You can create intentional microclimates by planting clusters of shrubs, trees, and ground covers that offer protection and create a favorable environment for seedlings.
- Mulching: Apply a thick layer of mulch around the planting areas. Mulch conserves moisture, reduces weeds, and gradually adds organic matter to the soil, benefiting seedlings and newly sprouted plants.

4. Direct Sowing vs. Indoor Seed Starting

Food forests can accommodate both direct sowing and indoor seed starting, each with unique advantages.

- Direct Sowing: Directly planting seeds in the ground is often more suitable for a food forest since it allows plants to grow in place, leading to stronger root systems. Direct sowing is particularly effective for hardy plants, ground covers, and certain nitrogen-fixers. To protect directly sown seeds from being washed away or eaten, you might use mulch, row covers, or even strategically place fallen branches.
- Indoor Seed Starting: Some plants require a longer growing season or warmer conditions to germinate and establish before they can be safely transplanted outdoors. For tender plants like tomatoes or certain herbs, indoor seed starting can be beneficial. Seedlings are typically started indoors several weeks before the last frost and later transplanted to their designated spots in the food forest.

When transplanting seedlings, it's important to "harden them off" by gradually exposing them to outdoor conditions, preventing transplant shock. In a food forest, the microclimates provided by other plants often make this process easier.

5. Natural Seed Germination Techniques

Food forest designs often take advantage of natural germination processes that mimic wild plant life cycles, including methods like:

- Cold Stratification: Certain seeds, particularly from trees and shrubs, require a period of cold to break dormancy. This process can be achieved by planting seeds in the fall or by artificially stratifying them in a refrigerator before planting in spring.
- Scarification: Some seeds have hard coats that need to be worn down for germination, either through a process that occurs naturally in soil over time or manually by lightly sanding or nicking the seed coat.
- Self-Seeding: Allowing certain plants to self-seed encourages the development of a perennial food forest that re-grows each year. For example, plants like borage, calendula, and certain grains will drop seeds that germinate naturally, providing food, ground cover, and habitat for wildlife.

6. Maintaining Seedlings and Young Plants

Once seeds have germinated, maintenance focuses on ensuring that seedlings establish themselves without heavy intervention:

- Watering: Young plants benefit from regular but moderate watering, especially during dry spells. Mulch helps retain soil moisture, reducing the frequency of watering.
- Weeding: Ground cover plants can reduce weed pressure, but early in a plant's life, it may still be necessary to remove competing weeds nearby. Adding nitrogen-fixing plants as companion plants enriches the soil and supports seedlings.
- Observation and Adaptation: A food forest is a dynamic system that requires continuous observation. Some plants may not perform as expected, prompting adjustments to spacing, plant combinations, or succession timing. Certain plants may naturally "volunteer" (self-seed) in areas, and allowing these volunteers to thrive can lead to unexpected but beneficial plant communities.

7. The Long-Term Benefits of Seed Starting in a Food Forest

Seed starting contributes to the long-term resilience of a food forest. By beginning with diverse seed selections and natural germination techniques, the forest becomes self-replicating and adaptive over time. The root systems of plants started from seeds are often stronger and more resilient than transplanted specimens, which can lead to greater drought tolerance and deeper nutrient access. Additionally, allowing plants to self-seed and establishing a natural cycle of succession planting encourages biodiversity, soil health, and an ecosystem capable of withstanding various environmental stresses.

In sum, seed starting in a food forest is an investment in a sustainable, productive ecosystem. Through mindful seed selection, timing, site preparation, and natural germination, a food forest can thrive as a low-maintenance, regenerative landscape that mimics natural processes while providing food, habitat, and ecological benefits.

GRAFTING

Grafting is a propagation technique where a branch or bud from one plant (the scion) is attached to the root system of another plant (the rootstock). This method combines desirable traits from two different plants, allowing gardeners and food foresters to propagate exact clones of a specific variety on a hardy, adaptable rootstock. Grafting is especially common in fruit tree propagation because it ensures fruit consistency, disease resistance, and greater adaptability to different soils and climates. Here's a comprehensive discussion of grafting procedures, including popular grafting methods, step-by-step instructions, and ideal applications.

Understanding Key Grafting Components and Terms

- Scion: A small piece of a plant, usually containing 2-4 buds, that will grow into the upper part of the grafted plant.
- Rootstock: The plant providing the root system. Rootstocks are chosen for their hardiness, disease resistance, or compatibility with specific soil types.
- Cambium Layer: A thin layer of actively growing cells located just beneath the bark. For successful grafting, the cambium layers of the scion and rootstock must align and join, as this is where new growth will occur.
- Union: The point where the scion and rootstock are joined.

Popular Grafting Techniques

Each grafting method has unique advantages, and choosing the right one depends on factors like plant species, grafting season, and the size of the scion and rootstock.

A. Whip-and-Tongue Graft

This grafting technique is ideal for small fruit trees, such as apple and pear trees, especially when the rootstock and scion are similar in diameter. It's one of the most secure graft types due to the "tongue" cut, which provides an extensive contact area between the scion and rootstock, ensuring precise cambium alignment and improving the likelihood of a successful graft.

Step-by-Step

1. Cut the Rootstock: Cut a straight, sloping cut on the rootstock, about 1-2 inches long.

2. Make the Tongue: Make a small cut on the slope to create a "tongue." This tongue will help lock the scion and rootstock together.

3. Prepare the Scion: Cut the base of the scion to match the slope of the rootstock, creating a similar tongue cut.

4. Join the Pieces: Slide the scion and rootstock together so the tongues interlock and the cambium layers match up.

5. Secure the Graft: Wrap the graft with grafting tape or rubber bands, then seal it with grafting wax to prevent drying.

B. Cleft Graft

This grafting method is highly effective for small fruit trees, including apple and pear varieties, particularly when the rootstock and scion are of similar diameter. Known for its reliability, this approach uses a "tongue" cut, creating a broad contact area that promotes strong cambium alignment. This design increases the chances of a successful graft by enhancing the structural stability and nutrient transfer between the scion and rootstock.

Procedure

1. Prepare the Rootstock: Cut the rootstock horizontally and split it down the center, about 1-2 inches deep.
2. Prepare the Scion: Cut the scion into a wedge shape, ensuring both sides taper evenly to maximize cambium contact.
3. Insert the Scion: Place the scion wedge into the cleft of the rootstock so that the cambium layers on at least one side are aligned.
4. Secure and Seal: Wrap the graft area with grafting tape or rubber bands, then apply grafting wax to seal and protect the cut area.

C. Budding (Bud Graft)

This grafting method is ideal when scion wood is scarce, particularly for young trees like apples, cherries, and peaches. By using a single bud instead of an entire branch, it provides a quicker and more resource-efficient grafting option, conserving scion material while still establishing a strong union between the scion and rootstock.

Procedure

1. Prepare the Rootstock: Make a T-shaped cut in the rootstock bark.
2. Prepare the Bud: Cut a single, healthy bud from the scion with a small shield of bark and cambium.

3. Insert the Bud: Slide the bud shield under the T-cut bark flaps, aligning the cambium layers.

4. Secure the Bud: Wrap the area with grafting tape to hold the bud in place and protect it as it heals.

D. Approach Graft

This grafting method is especially useful for nut trees and delicate plants, where both the scion and rootstock remain attached to their original plants and continue to grow until the graft takes. By allowing both parts to receive nutrients from their own root systems throughout the healing process, this technique supports healthier graft establishment in actively growing plants.

Procedure:

1. Choose Healthy Branches: Select a branch from each plant (rootstock and scion) that are close in size.

2. Make Matching Cuts: On each plant, make a shallow cut that matches the other, exposing the cambium layers.

3. Join the Cuts: Align the cuts and tie the two branches together with grafting tape or a rubber band.

4. Allow Time to Heal: Let the graft heal over several weeks, then cut away the scion from its original rootstock, allowing it to rely on the new rootstock.

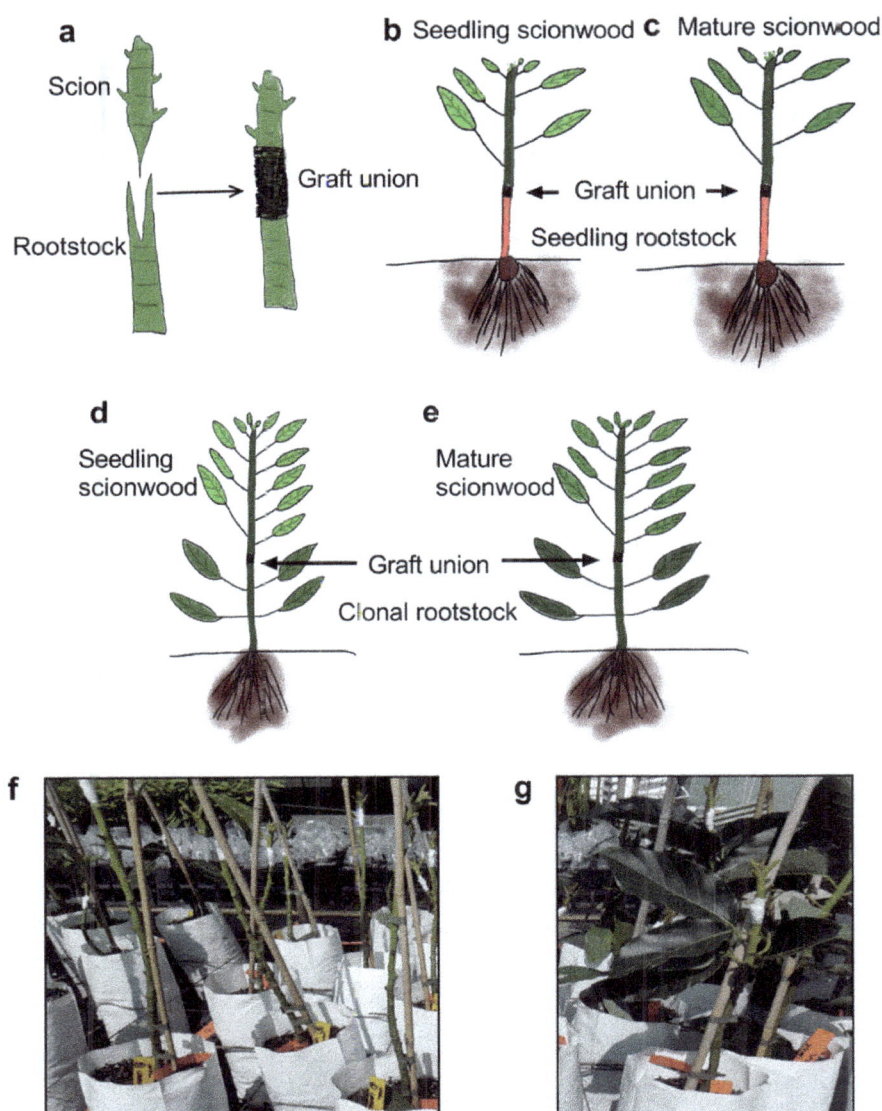

Grafting Aftercare and Success Tips

Aftercare is essential for successful grafting, regardless of the method used. Protecting the graft union from sun and moisture loss with grafting wax or tape prevents it from drying out. Removing competing shoots from the rootstock ensures that nutrients and energy are directed to the grafted scion. After several weeks, inspect the graft for new growth and callus formation, signs that the graft has successfully taken. In methods like approach grafting, gradually reducing the original connection allows the scion to adjust smoothly to the new rootstock.

Benefits and Applications of Grafting in a Food Forest

Grafting provides multiple benefits for food foresters. It preserves desirable traits by replicating trees with specific fruit qualities, hardiness, or disease resistance. Grafted trees reach maturity faster than those grown from seed, leading to quicker harvests. Grafting also enhances diversity, allowing multiple varieties to grow on the same rootstock, which saves space and creates a richer food forest. Additionally, by using a hardy rootstock, grafted plants can adapt more effectively to challenging soil or climate conditions, supporting resilience in various environments. With practice, grafting allows food foresters to enhance the diversity, productivity, and resilience of a food forest. It's a valuable technique that combines botanical knowledge with craftsmanship to create sustainable food systems that thrive for generations.

CUTTINGS

Taking cuttings is a highly effective propagation method in a food forest, enabling the rapid establishment of diverse, resilient layers in the ecosystem. By growing new plants from segments of existing ones—such as stems, leaves, or roots—food foresters can quickly add genetically identical plants with desirable traits, such as high productivity, disease resistance, or specific growth habits, to the forest. This method requires fewer resources than seed-starting and allows for reliable replication of the parent plant's characteristics, ensuring consistency in qualities like fruit quality and pest resistance.

In this process, cuttings are removed from a parent plant and encouraged to develop roots, forming independent plants that are direct clones of their source. Several types of cuttings can be used, each suited to different species and seasons. Softwood cuttings, taken from new, flexible growth in spring or early summer, are ideal for herbs, berries, and certain shrubs. Semi-hardwood cuttings, which come from partially matured growth later in the season, work well for plants like rosemary and blueberries. Hardwood cuttings, gathered from woody, dormant branches in fall or winter, are best suited for fruit-bearing trees like grapes, apples, and mulberries. Leaf cuttings and root cuttings, although less common, are excellent for herbs and certain root-based plants.

Each type of cutting follows a basic procedure tailored to its specific needs, such as making clean cuts below nodes, applying rooting hormones, planting in well-draining mediums, and maintaining humidity to encourage root growth. Through these techniques, food foresters can cultivate a wide variety of plants, from shrubs and groundcovers to canopy trees, all while promoting genetic consistency, biodiversity, and rapid growth within their food forest. This propagation strategy not only accelerates the establishment of a self-sustaining forest ecosystem but also fosters a rich diversity of species that contribute to the food forest's productivity and ecological resilience.

Types of Cuttings and Their Procedures

Each type of cutting has unique requirements, depending on the plant's growth habits, season, and root-forming tendencies. Here are the primary types of cuttings:

A. Softwood Cuttings

Softwood cuttings work well for deciduous trees, shrubs, and herbaceous plants during the early growing season, typically from spring to early summer. This method is especially effective for plants like elderberries, currants, gooseberries, figs, blackberries, and certain herbs such as mint and basil.

Procedure

1.Select a Healthy Shoot: Choose a fresh, flexible stem (softwood) from the current season's growth, about 4-6 inches long.

2. Remove Lower Leaves: Trim the bottom leaves, leaving only a few leaves at the top to reduce water loss.

3. Prepare the Cutting**: Make a clean cut just below a leaf node, where roots are more likely to form.

4. Apply Rooting Hormone: Dip the cut end in rooting hormone to encourage faster root development.

5. Plant the Cutting: Insert the cutting into a well-draining, moist growing medium like a mix of sand and peat or perlite.

6. Maintain High Humidity: Cover with a plastic dome or bag to maintain humidity. Place in indirect light.

7. Monitor and Mist: Keep the medium moist, and within 2-4 weeks, softwood cuttings usually start forming roots.

B. Semi-Hardwood Cuttings

Semi-hardwood cuttings are best suited for trees and shrubs during late summer, a time when their growth has matured slightly but is not fully woody. This stage in the plant's life cycle provides an ideal balance between flexibility and sturdiness, making it easier for the cuttings to root successfully. Common examples of plants that propagate well from semi-hardwood cuttings include blueberries, rosemary, sage, olive, and certain fruit trees like apples and pears. This method is especially effective for species that benefit from late-season growth, enabling food forest gardeners to expand their plant diversity with resilient, well-established specimens.

Procedure

1. Select a Semi-Mature Stem: Cut 4-6 inches of semi-hardwood from the current season's mature, yet pliable, growth.

2. Trim Leaves: Remove leaves from the lower half of the cutting to reduce moisture loss.

3. Make a Clean Cut Below a Node: Nodes, where leaves or buds meet the stem, are ideal rooting points.

4. Use Rooting Hormone (Recommended): Dip the cut end into rooting hormone, as semi-hardwood cuttings may root more slowly.

5. Plant and Cover: Place the cutting in a well-draining, moist growing medium, and cover it with a humidity dome or plastic to retain moisture.

6. Provide Indirect Light: Place the cutting in a bright, but indirect light source.

7. Wait for Root Development: Semi-hardwood cuttings may take 6-12 weeks to root, so be patient and monitor the moisture level.

C. Hardwood Cuttings

Hardwood cuttings are ideal for propagating woody plants and trees during their dormant season, typically from late fall to winter. At this stage, plants are less active, which reduces stress on the cuttings and increases their likelihood of successfully rooting. This method works well for a variety of woody species, including grape vines, apples, pears, plums, mulberries, and elderberries, allowing food forest gardeners to efficiently reproduce these plants during a time when other gardening tasks may be minimal. By taking hardwood cuttings in the dormant season, gardeners can establish new plants that will thrive and contribute to the food forest's growth and resilience.

Procedure

1. Choose Dormant Wood: Select healthy, leafless branches from the previous season's growth, typically 8-12 inches long.

2. Remove Extra Branches: Trim off side branches and any leaves (though most are usually gone in winter).

3. Cut Just Below a Node: Make the bottom cut just below a node to encourage root formation.

4. Dip in Rooting Hormone: Although optional, it's helpful for hardwood cuttings as they root more slowly.

5. Plant in Soil or a Growing Bed: Stick the cutting into the ground or a pot with well-draining soil. Place most of the cutting below the soil surface, with one or two nodes above ground.

6. Provide Winter Protection: In cold climates, cover with mulch or plant in a sheltered area. Hardwood cuttings take several months to root, often emerging in spring.

D. Leaf Cuttings

Leaf cuttings are an effective propagation method for certain herbs, houseplants, and succulents capable of rooting from leaf tissue. This technique is especially suitable for plants like strawberries, comfrey, rhubarb, and various mints and sages, which can develop new roots and shoots from their leaves. By using leaf cuttings, food forest gardeners can easily expand their plant diversity, particularly among ground covers and herbaceous plants, enhancing soil health, moisture retention, and biodiversity within the ecosystem.

Procedure

1. Choose a Healthy Leaf: For plants like comfrey or rhubarb, choose a fresh, mature leaf with a petiole (leaf stem).

2. Cut the Leaf and Prepare: For rhubarb, place the base in water; for strawberries, plant the petiole in soil.

3. Place in Moist Medium: Insert the cut end into a potting mix.

4. Maintain Humidity: Keep the medium moist and place the leaf in indirect light.

5. Monitor for Root Growth: Leaf cuttings often root within 2-6 weeks, depending on the plant.

E. Root Cuttings

Root cuttings are a useful propagation method for perennials that naturally form roots from segments, making them especially effective for plants like horseradish, raspberries, blackberries, and certain herbs such as mint and comfrey. This technique involves taking sections of the root to produce new plants, which is ideal for expanding root vegetable patches and perennial herbs in a food forest.

Procedure

1. Select a Root Segment: Dig up a section of healthy root, about 2-4 inches long.
2. Plant in Soil: Bury the root horizontally or vertically, depending on the plant.
3. Cover with Soil: Ensure the soil is well-draining but rich in nutrients.
4. Water Regularly: Keep the soil consistently moist to encourage root and shoot development.

Best Practices for Successful Cuttings in a Food Forest

Successful propagation from cuttings in a food forest depends on several key practices that optimize rooting conditions and prevent disease. Choosing the correct season for each type of cutting is crucial—softwood in spring, hardwood in winter, and so on—to match the plant's growth stage with rooting needs. Sterilizing tools helps prevent disease transfer, maintaining the health of both parent plants and new cuttings. Humidity control is essential, as high moisture levels prevent cuttings from drying out while rooting; using plastic covers or regular misting helps maintain this environment. Although optional, applying rooting hormone can significantly increase rooting success, particularly for more challenging cuttings like semi-hardwood and hardwood. Selecting a well-draining medium, such as a mix of sand, peat, and perlite, prevents waterlogging and root rot. Finally, labeling each cutting is important when propagating multiple species, allowing for easy identification and management as the plants establish themselves in the food forest.

Benefits of Cuttings in a Food Forest

Making use of cuttings for propagation in a food forest offers several key advantages that support efficient and sustainable ecosystem development. Cuttings produce genetically consistent plants that are identical to the parent, preserving valuable traits like disease resistance and high fruit quality. This method also allows for rapid establishment, especially with softwood and semi-hardwood cuttings, which root quickly and accelerate forest growth. Cuttings are cost-effective, reducing the need to purchase new plants or seeds and making it easy to share resources within communities. Additionally, by propagating cuttings across different layers—canopy, understory, and shrub—food forests can quickly diversify, creating a rich, multi-layered environment that closely resembles natural ecosystems.

Examples of Planting and Using Cuttings in a Food Forest

Using cuttings to propagate plants in a food forest is a sustainable, low-cost approach that accelerates growth and enhances biodiversity across multiple layers of the ecosystem. Carefully chosen cuttings contribute to a self-sustaining forest by filling diverse roles. For example, elderberries and currants ideal for semi-hardwood or hardwood cuttings, establish productive shrub layers that yield fruit and attract pollinators. Herbaceous plants like mint and oregano root easily from stem cuttings, providing excellent ground cover and protecting soil health. Grapes and figs, propagated from hardwood cuttings, add a vertical layer and produce abundant fruit, while root cuttings of raspberries and blackberries can quickly expand berry patches, serving as both food sources and natural barriers. By integrating these species through cuttings, food forest practitioners build resilient ecosystems that offer continuous yields of food, medicinal resources, and habitat for wildlife, fostering a balanced and thriving forest environment.

PLANTING TECHNIQUES AND SPACING

Planting techniques and spacing are foundational elements in food forest design, essential for creating a balanced, productive ecosystem that mimics natural forests. The arrangement and spacing of plants directly affect sunlight, soil health, water usage, and overall plant productivity. In a food forest, the goal is to establish multiple plant layers—canopy, understory, shrub, herbaceous, ground cover, root, and vine layers—to create a dense, diverse environment. Below is a detailed look at planting techniques, optimal spacing, and practical examples that illustrate these principles.

Layering Plants by Function and Height

In food forests, planting each layer with the right spacing creates a dynamic environment where plants can support one another without competing excessively for resources. In a food forest, effective planting and spacing are crucial for creating a balanced ecosystem where each layer of vegetation plays a distinct role. At the highest level, the canopy layer consists of tall trees like walnuts, chestnuts, and apples, which provide essential shade and act as windbreaks. These trees require the largest spacing, often 30-40 feet for species like chestnut, to allow their expansive roots and canopies to develop without overcrowding nearby trees.

Below the canopy is the understory layer, which includes smaller trees such as persimmons and mulberries. These trees, spaced closer than canopy trees—typically around 15-20 feet apart—thrive in the partial shade created by the canopy. For example, persimmons benefit from growing under tall, open-canopied trees like walnuts, which allow them access to filtered sunlight

The shrub layer occupies the space beneath the trees and provides fruits, habitats for wildlife, and support for beneficial insects. Shrubs like elderberries and currants are ideal for this layer, with elderberries needing about 8 feet of spacing due to their tendency to spread, while smaller shrubs like currants can be spaced closer together, around 3-5 feet. Each layer contributes to a cohesive and productive food forest ecosystem, with well-planned spacing ensuring that every plant can thrive and fulfill its ecological role.

Companion Planting and Guilds

Companion planting as earlier discussed involves pairing plants that benefit each other, either by improving soil fertility, deterring pests, or enhancing pollination. Guilds, a more structured form of companion planting, are groups of plants that perform complementary roles. In a food forest, utilizing plant guilds enhances biodiversity and productivity by pairing complementary species that support each other's growth. One well-known example is the Apple Tree Guild, which features an apple tree accompanied by nitrogen-fixing plants like clover or lupine to enrich the soil. Additionally, garlic or chives are included for their pest-repelling properties, while borage attracts beneficial pollinators. These companion plants can be interspersed within a 3-5 foot radius of the apple tree, which is typically spaced 20-30 feet from other trees, maximizing their synergistic benefits.

Another effective guild is the Three Sisters Guild, comprising corn, beans, and squash. In this arrangement, corn serves as a natural trellis for the climbing beans, which fix nitrogen in the soil, enhancing fertility for all three plants. Meanwhile, the squash acts as a living mulch, suppressing weeds and retaining soil moisture. The Three Sisters require less spacing than other guilds, with a typical arrangement of about 3-4 feet per "hill" or group, making it an efficient choice for smaller areas within the food forest. Together, these guilds illustrate the importance of strategic planting in creating a thriving, interconnected ecosystem.

High-Density Planting for Perennial Herbs and Ground Covers

High-density planting is often used with ground covers and low-growing herbs that fill in gaps, improve soil health, and reduce weeds. This technique involves planting these species more closely together to establish a dense ground cover. For instances Creeping thyme, mint, and oregano are excellent ground covers that spread quickly and only need a few inches of spacing when first planted. These can be interspersed among larger plants, filling gaps and helping to conserve moisture in the soil. For instance, 6-8 inches of spacing between thyme plants will soon form a thick mat.

Root Layer and Root Spacing Techniques

The root layer includes plants that grow primarily underground, and their spacing is key to preventing competition with trees and shrubs. For examples Plants like horseradish, sunchokes, and garlic can thrive in the root layer. Horseradish, which spreads through root runners, should be planted about 1-2 feet apart from other root crops. Garlic, which is smaller, can be spaced around 6 inches apart and is often planted in clusters around fruit trees to repel pests.

Vining Layer and Vertical Spacing

Vines utilize vertical space, which is often underused in food forests, allowing for increased productivity without expanding horizontally. An example is using Grapes and kiwis which are excellent vine choices that can climb or trees or trellises. Grapes, when trellised, should be spaced 6-8 feet apart, but if allowed to climb a host tree like a walnut or mulberry, spacing considerations shift toward managing their pruning and growth. Vines can also grow on tall shrubs or man-made structures, adding to the layered effect without requiring much ground area.

Cluster and Staggered Spacing

Cluster planting, or planting in small, dense groups, can mimic natural growth patterns and promote resource sharing among plants. In a mixed berry patch with raspberries and blackberries, spacing each cluster 2-3 feet apart within rows but staggering clusters from row to row allows them to establish dense patches that prevent weeds and provide abundant harvests.

Microclimate Considerations and Spacing Adjustments

In a food forest, spacing can be adjusted to create microclimates, which are small areas with distinct climate conditions within the forest. Close spacing of taller trees and shrubs can create shaded, cooler areas for shade-loving plants. Planting nut trees like walnuts or pecans with elderberries and currants nearby can create a shaded understory. The cooler microclimate is ideal for moisture-loving plants like mint or comfrey, which can grow with closer spacing here than they would in an open, sunny area.

Spacing for Accessibility and Harvest

Spacing should also accommodate human access for maintenance and harvesting. Paths can be integrated by spacing shrubs and trees with gaps or rows wide enough for easy movement. In an apple tree guild, for instance, pathways around trees and shrub layers (like currants or gooseberries) spaced in an alternating pattern help ensure that the fruit can be easily reached from both the canopy and understory levels.

An effective planting technique and careful spacing create a thriving, balanced food forest where each plant layer supports the others. By considering factors like plant height, root spread, companion relationships, and microclimate needs, food forest practitioners can maximize productivity, reduce competition, and encourage resilience within the forest ecosystem. These approaches foster a dense, multi-layered environment that not only yields diverse food but also nurtures a stable habitat for wildlife and beneficial insects, contributing to the overall health and sustainability of the food forest.

TRANSPLANTING AND AFTERCARE

Transplanting is a vital process in the establishment and management of a food forest. It involves moving plants from one location to another to ensure they thrive in optimal conditions, contribute to biodiversity, and maximize productivity. This comprehensive discussion will outline the steps involved in transplanting, the best practices to follow, and the considerations to keep in mind, supported by vivid illustrations of the techniques and their applications.

Transplanting

Transplanting in a food forest involves moving seedlings, young trees, or established plants to a new location within the forest. This process is undertaken for several reasons, including creating space to promote better growth and resource access, adjusting to microclimates that offer more suitable conditions for specific plants, and enhancing biodiversity by introducing new species that support a diverse ecosystem.

Timing for Transplanting

Timing is crucial for successful transplanting in a food forest, with the best period typically occurring during a plant's dormant season, which is usually in late fall or early spring. During these times, plants experience less stress and can concentrate their energy on establishing roots rather than producing leaves or fruits. For example, deciduous trees such as apple and pear trees should ideally be transplanted in late winter before they begin to bud, while perennials like comfrey and raspberries can be moved in early spring as they start to grow. This careful timing ensures a higher survival rate and promotes healthy development in their new locations.

Preparing for Transplanting

When preparing for transplanting in a food forest, the first step is to select healthy plants that are well-suited to your ecosystem, taking into account their specific growth requirements such as light, water, and soil conditions. Next, prepare the new planting site by amending the soil with organic matter like compost to enhance nutrient content and improve drainage. It's essential to plan for adequate spacing based on the mature size of the plants to prevent overcrowding, ensuring that each plant has enough room to thrive in its new location. This thoughtful preparation promotes successful transplantation and supports the overall health of the food forest.

The Transplanting Process

- **Watering Before Transplanting:** Water the plant thoroughly the day before transplanting to reduce transplant shock and ensure the soil is moist.

- **Digging Up the Plant:** To successfully transplant a plant, use a spade or shovel to dig around it while keeping as much of the root system intact as possible. A general guideline is to create a hole that is at least twice the width of the root ball to facilitate a healthy transplant. For example, picture a young apple tree being gently lifted from the ground, with its roots preserved as the gardener carefully digs a wide circle around it to avoid any damage. This technique ensures that the plant has the best chance of thriving in its new location.

- **Transporting the Plant:** Carefully transport the plant to the new location. For larger plants or trees, use a wheelbarrow or carry it by the root ball to minimize stress on the roots.
- **Planting in the New Location:** When transplanting a plant, begin by digging a planting hole in the new location that is slightly deeper than the root ball and at least twice as wide. Next, position the plant in the center of the hole, ensuring that the top of the root ball is level with or slightly above the surrounding soil to allow for settling. After positioning, gently backfill around the root ball with the original soil, taking care to remove any air pockets by lightly tamping it down. Finally, water the area thoroughly to help settle the soil around the roots, promoting healthy establishment in the new location.

Transplanting Examples in a Food Forest

When transplanting in a food forest, it's important to consider the specific spacing requirements for different types of plants. For fruit trees like apple and pear trees, ensure they are spaced adequately—about 20-30 feet apart—to accommodate their mature canopy size. For example, when moving a young apple tree, enrich the surrounding soil with compost to promote healthy growth. In contrast, when transplanting herbs such as mint or oregano, which can enhance ground cover, space them about 1-2 feet apart to allow for their spreading nature. Similarly, when relocating raspberry or blackberry plants, cluster them in groups spaced 2-3 feet apart to create a dense berry patch that provides both food and habitat. This thoughtful approach to spacing ensures each plant thrives in its new environment while contributing to the overall health and productivity of the food forest.

Transplanting is an essential practice in a food forest that contributes to plant health, ecosystem diversity, and overall productivity. By carefully selecting plants, timing the process correctly, and following proper transplanting techniques, gardeners can successfully move plants within their food forest, ensuring they thrive in their new environment. With attention to post-transplant care, the benefits of a well-planned transplanting strategy will foster a thriving, resilient food forest ecosystem that continues to yield food, medicine, and habitat for years to come.

AFTERCARE

Effective aftercare following plant transplanting in a food forest is crucial for ensuring their establishment, resilience, and long-term health. Newly transplanted plants face significant stress as they adapt to their new environment and establish roots, making watering essential. Immediately after transplanting, thorough watering settles the soil around roots, removing air pockets to ensure good soil-root contact. Ongoing deep watering in the first few weeks maintains consistent moisture, supporting the root system without risking root rot.

Mulching provides further support by retaining soil moisture, suppressing weeds, and stabilizing soil temperatures. A 2-4 inch layer of organic mulch, like wood chips or straw, around the plant base (but not touching the stem) helps reduce watering frequency, limits weed competition, and shields roots from extreme temperatures. Regular monitoring then becomes vital for detecting early signs of pests, disease, or stress, such as leaf drop or wilting, so gardeners can take prompt action if needed. Healthy growth is a positive sign of acclimation, indicating the plant's adjustment to its new location.

For some newly transplanted trees and shrubs, pruning damaged or diseased branches redirects energy to healthy growth, and light shaping (especially for fruit trees) helps establish a strong structure. However, heavy pruning should be avoided to minimize stress. Additionally, fertilizing with organic options like compost or well-rotted manure provides balanced nutrients without overwhelming roots. A slow-release, balanced fertilizer in spring offers steady nutrition, but over-fertilizing should be avoided to prevent root damage.

Creating a supportive growth environment is equally important. Companion planting introduces beneficial plants nearby, such as nitrogen-fixing legumes that enrich soil, while flowering plants attract pollinators to support fruit set and plant health. Lastly, patience and observation play key roles. Transplanted plants need time to adjust, with root establishment typically taking several weeks to months. Seasonal adjustments, such as increased watering during dry spells or adjusting mulch thickness, accommodate plants' changing needs through the growing season. Integrating these practices—watering, mulching, monitoring, pruning fertilizing, companion planting, and careful observation gardeners can support individual plant resilience and contribute to the food forest's biodiversity, productivity, and ecological health, fostering a thriving, self-sustaining ecosystem.

CHAPTER SIX

FOOD FOREST MANAGEMENT

THE FUNGAL LAYER

In a food forest, the fungal layer is essential to maintaining soil health, nutrient cycling, and ecosystem resilience. This layer, predominantly comprising mycorrhizal, saprophytic, and endophytic fungi, forms a symbiotic network with plants and trees, supporting growth and soil health through complex relationships.

Mycorrhizal fungi are central to this layer, establishing mutualistic bonds with plant roots that enhance nutrient exchange. These fungi come in two primary types: Arbuscular Mycorrhizal Fungi (AMF), which penetrate root cells to facilitate nutrient flow, and Ectomycorrhizal Fungi, which form a sheath around root cells and are typically associated with trees like oak, beech, and pine. Meanwhile, saprophytic fungi decompose dead organic material, recycling nutrients back into the soil, and endophytic fungi reside within plant tissues, often bolstering the plants' resistance to pests and diseases.

The benefits of this fungal layer are numerous. For nutrient cycling and soil fertility, mycorrhizal fungi expand plant root systems, allowing access to nutrients like phosphorus, nitrogen, and trace minerals. Saprophytic fungi assist by decomposing organic material, enriching the soil, while fungi-produced glomalin binds soil particles to improve structure and water retention, creating an ideal environment for root growth. In terms of water retention and drought resistance, the extensive hyphal networks of mycorrhizal fungi form a web that acts like a sponge, absorbing and retaining water within the soil and enhancing plant drought tolerance by extending their reach to moisture beyond the root zone.

Fungi also bolster disease resistance and plant health. Mycorrhizal fungi create a protective barrier around roots, shielding plants from soil-borne pathogens, while some fungi produce compounds that inhibit harmful soil microbes. Additionally, endophytic fungi in plant tissues produce compounds that deter herbivores and increase tolerance to environmental stresses like heat. This interconnected fungal layer supports biodiversity and ecosystem resilience by linking various plants, allowing them to share resources, which promotes plant diversity and strengthens ecosystem stability. Fungi also nourish a rich soil food web by serving as food for soil organisms, including bacteria, nematodes, and insects, which, in turn, contribute to a balanced ecosystem.

Furthermore, fungi aid in carbon sequestration, with mycorrhizal networks transferring carbon from plants to the soil, storing it in stable forms that help mitigate climate change. Saprophytic fungi contribute to long-term carbon storage by incorporating decomposed organic material into humus, which holds carbon for extended periods. To establish and enhance the fungal layer in a food forest, specific practices encourage fungal growth and support ecosystem balance. Regularly adding organic matter like compost, leaf litter, and wood chips promotes fungal growth and nutrient cycling, while minimizing soil disturbance helps fungi thrive. Organic practices should replace chemical inputs such as pesticides and fungicides, which can disrupt fungal networks. Incorporating diverse plant species, especially those compatible with mycorrhizal fungi, supports a more complex fungal network. Encouraging natural decay by leaving fallen branches and leaves on the ground also provides essential habitat and nutrients for saprophytic fungi. The fungal layer is vital to food forest health, enabling nutrient cycling, disease resistance, water retention, and carbon sequestration. By fostering fungal growth and respecting the interdependence between plants and fungi, food forest gardeners can create resilient, self-sustaining ecosystems that benefit plants, wildlife, and the surrounding environment.

MAXIMIZING THE FUNGAL LAYER

Maximizing the fungal layer in a food forest is essential for promoting soil health, nutrient availability, water retention, and overall ecosystem resilience. By cultivating an environment that encourages fungal growth and diversity, a food forest can become more self-sustaining and productive. Here's an in-depth look at techniques and best practices to maximize the fungal layer in a food forest:

Increase Organic Matter Inputs
Fungi thrive in soil rich in organic matter, as it provides food and habitat. Adding a variety of organic materials helps to create a stable food web where fungi play a central role.

- **Mulching with Wood Chips:** Wood chips, especially hardwood chips, are excellent for promoting fungal growth. As they decompose, they provide a long-term food source for saprophytic fungi. Apply a thick layer of wood chips (2-4 inches) around plants, particularly under trees and shrubs, to mimic the forest floor and promote mycorrhizal networks.
- **Incorporate Leaf Litter:** In natural forests, leaves fall and accumulate, forming a rich layer of organic material that feeds fungal networks. Collecting and spreading leaf litter around the food forest

helps replicate this natural cycle, fostering fungi that specialize in breaking down leaves.

- **Use Compost and Manure Sparingly:** While compost and manure primarily boost bacterial growth, adding a small amount mixed with wood chips or leaf litter provides balanced nutrition, supporting fungi without overwhelming their environment with bacteria.

Minimize Soil Disturbance

Fungal networks, especially mycorrhizal fungi, are delicate and can be damaged by excessive soil disturbance.

- **Reduce Tilling:** Avoid tilling or digging in areas where fungal networks are established, as this disrupts the hyphal networks that connect plant roots. Instead of tilling, use no-till methods like sheet mulching to build soil without disturbing fungi.
- **Spot Planting:** Instead of large-scale digging, plant new plants by creating small planting holes, minimizing the impact on established fungal colonies. Spot planting ensures that the fungal network remains mostly intact.

Encourage Mycorrhizal Fungi

Mycorrhizal fungi form mutually beneficial relationships with most plants, especially trees and perennials, providing nutrients in exchange for sugars from the plants.

- **Introduce Mycorrhizal Spores:** Adding mycorrhizal inoculants at planting can help establish beneficial fungi, especially in disturbed or newly established areas. This is particularly useful for fruit trees and perennial plants, which benefit greatly from mycorrhizal associations.

- **Select Mycorrhizal-Friendly Plants:** Some plants, especially perennials, trees, and shrubs, have a high affinity for mycorrhizal fungi. Species like oaks, chestnuts, apples, and elderberries naturally support and encourage mycorrhizal fungi, so planting these trees helps build a fungal-friendly environment.

Provide Decaying Wood and Log Hubs

Dead wood offers a perfect habitat for various types of saprophytic fungi, which decompose organic material and contribute to the nutrient cycle.

- **Establish Decay Zones:** Place logs, branches, and stumps in designated areas of the food forest to encourage fungi that specialize in wood decomposition. Over time, these decay zones enrich the soil and provide a habitat for mushrooms and other fungi.
- **Use Hugelkultur Beds:** Hugelkultur beds, which are made by burying logs under soil and organic matter, provide a long-term food source for fungi as the wood breaks down. These beds promote fungal dominance, improve water retention, and offer a fertile environment for plants.

Support Diverse Fungal Types Through Plant Diversity

Different plants support different fungi, so maximizing plant diversity encourages a variety of fungal species.

- **Plant a Range of Trees, Shrubs, and Herbs:** Aim for a variety of plants that attract both arbuscular and ectomycorrhizal fungi. For example, pairing trees like chestnuts and pines (which support ectomycorrhizal fungi) with herbaceous plants that support arbuscular fungi creates a diverse fungal community.

- **Add Perennials and Native Species:** Perennial plants create stable root systems that allow fungal networks to establish and thrive long-term. Native species are especially valuable, as they often have co-evolved relationships with local fungal species, providing a balanced and resilient fungal community.

Maintain Moisture Level

Fungi require consistent moisture to grow and establish themselves, especially during the establishment phase.

- **Use Mulch to Conserve Moisture:** A thick layer of organic mulch, such as wood chips or straw, helps retain moisture in the soil, creating an ideal environment for fungi. Mulch also acts as a slow-release food source as it breaks down.
- **Build Swales and Hugelkultur Beds:** Swales (shallow trenches that collect rainwater) and hugelkultur beds help capture and retain water, providing consistent moisture that supports fungal growth.
- **Shade Canopy:** Establishing a canopy layer in the food forest helps regulate temperature and retain soil moisture, creating a more stable environment for fungi.

Limit Chemical Inputs

Fungi are sensitive to synthetic chemicals, so minimizing or eliminating these inputs is essential.

- **Avoid Fungicides and Synthetic Fertilizers:** Fungicides are directly harmful to beneficial fungi, while synthetic fertilizers can disrupt the soil's natural nutrient balance, reducing the need for mycorrhizal relationships. Instead, use organic soil amendments that support a balanced soil microbiome.
- **Reduce Pesticide Use:** Some pesticides harm the broader soil ecosystem, impacting both fungi and the organisms that interact with them. Integrated pest management practices, such as planting pest-repelling plants or encouraging predator insects, offer alternative solutions.

Promote Fungi-Specific Amendments

Certain organic amendments support fungal growth specifically.

- **Biochar:** Biochar, a form of charcoal added to the soil, enhances soil structure, holds moisture, and provides a stable habitat for fungal growth. Biochar is especially effective in acidic or sandy soils where fungi may struggle to establish.
- **Mycelium-Rich Compost:** Adding compost that contains visible fungal growth, often called "fungally dominated compost," introduces beneficial fungi to the soil. This type of compost works well in areas where trees, shrubs, and other woody plants grow.

Allow Natural Succession and Fungal Development

Natural succession is the process by which an ecosystem gradually shifts over time, with fungi playing a key role in the early and mature stages.

- **Leave Some Areas Untouched:** Allowing parts of the food forest to remain undisturbed promotes natural fungal growth, as fallen leaves, branches, and other organic matter accumulate. Over time, these areas become hotspots of fungal activity and nutrient cycling.
- **Encourage Leaf Litter Accumulation:** Rather than removing leaves, let them decompose on the forest floor. This decomposition fosters a continuous cycle of nutrient return, which encourages fungal diversity and benefits the entire food forest.

Monitor and Observe Fungal Growth

Understanding how fungi are developing and spreading in a food forest helps in adjusting practices to better support them.

- **Observe Soil and Plant Health:** Healthy, mycorrhizal-rich soil tends to be crumbly and dark, with a pleasant, earthy smell. Plants with strong fungal connections will often show greater resilience to drought and pests.
- **Look for Mushrooms:** Fruiting bodies like mushrooms indicate that fungal networks are well-established. Seeing different species of mushrooms is a sign of a diverse fungal ecosystem, which is beneficial for nutrient cycling and soil health.

By using techniques that support the fungal layer, food forest practitioners can create a thriving, resilient system where fungi contribute to nutrient cycling, soil structure, water retention, and disease resistance. The fungal layer is integral to the food forest's self-sustaining ecosystem, promoting health from the roots up and maximizing productivity naturally.

PRUNING AND CARE

Pruning is essential in a food forest to encourage healthy growth, improve yields, manage plant size, and maintain the ecosystem's structure. Since food forests involve a variety of plant types—from fruit trees to shrubs and ground cover plants—each type requires specific pruning techniques. Here's an in-depth look at effective pruning techniques tailored to different plants in a food forest:

1. Pruning Fruit Trees

Fruit trees are a significant part of the canopy and understory layers in food forests. Pruning them ensures better light penetration, airflow, and fruit quality.

- **Formative Pruning:** In the first few years of a young tree's life, formative pruning is crucial for shaping its structure, minimizing weak branches, and encouraging a balanced canopy. The technique involves selecting a strong central leader (the main trunk) in the first winter and removing competing branches to establish a clear, dominant vertical structure. Remaining branches are cut back to create a symmetrical shape. For apple and pear trees, this approach emphasizes creating a central leader form with evenly spaced lateral branches, ensuring the tree grows upright and maintains a strong, stable structure.

- **Annual Maintenance Pruning:** Annual pruning in late winter or early spring is beneficial for mature fruit trees, as it removes deadwood, suckers (vigorous shoots from the base), and crossing branches. This process involves thinning the center of the tree to allow sunlight to penetrate and reach the lower branches, which enhances fruit quality. Additionally, overly long branches are shortened by cutting back to an outward-facing bud to control size and encourage balanced growth. For trees like peaches and plums, an open center form is particularly effective, as it maximizes light exposure throughout the canopy, reducing fungal diseases and improving overall fruit quality.

- **Rejuvenation Pruning:** For older or neglected trees, intensive pruning over several seasons can restore productivity by gradually encouraging new growth. This technique involves removing up to a third of old, unproductive branches each year, allowing the tree to regenerate without overwhelming it. In the case of old apple trees, priority is given to removing vertical shoots and overly dense branches within the canopy, which opens up the structure and promotes healthier, more manageable growth.

2. Pruning Berry Bushes

Berry bushes such as raspberries, blackberries, and currants are integral to the shrub layer in food forests, providing fruits and supporting biodiversity.

- **Cane Pruning (Raspberries and Blackberries):** These berries fruit on two-year-old canes, or biennial canes, making it important to understand their growth cycle for effective pruning. For summer-bearing varieties, pruning involves removing the canes that have already fruited, known as floricanes, immediately after harvest. This opens space for new growth, called primocanes, which will bear fruit the following year. For raspberries, this means cutting fruited canes back to ground level after harvest and spacing the remaining canes about 4-6 inches apart to improve air circulation and promote healthy growth.

- **Thinning and Rejuvenation (Currants and Gooseberries):** These berries produce fruit on older wood but benefit from selective removal of older branches to maintain bush health. The pruning technique involves removing the oldest, least productive stems each winter, leaving 8-12 strong, younger stems to ensure continued productivity. This thinning enhances airflow and light penetration within the bush, which helps reduce disease. For currants, specifically, removing stems older than three years encourages vigorous new growth and results in larger, healthier berries.

3. Pruning Nut Trees

Nut trees like chestnuts, hazelnuts, and walnuts form the upper canopy and generally require less intensive pruning.

- **Structural Pruning:** In the first few years, young trees should be guided to develop a strong central leader and a balanced structure by removing weak or competing branches. The technique involves eliminating side branches growing at sharp angles, as these are more prone to breakage, and establishing a single, dominant leader to encourage vertical growth. For trees like walnuts, it's essential to focus on creating this strong structure within the first 3-5 years, as mature walnut trees become challenging to prune effectively.
- **Light Thinning:** Once mature, nut trees require minimal pruning, but occasional thinning helps remove deadwood and low-hanging branches that may obstruct lower canopy layers. The technique

involves light thinning every few years to keep the canopy open, ensuring sunlight can reach other forest layers below. For example, hazelnuts benefit from periodic removal of dense growth to maintain their bush shape and improve air circulation, which helps reduce the risk of disease.

4. Pruning Shrubs and Medicinal Plants

Shrubs and perennial plants in food forests serve multiple functions, from providing habitat to attracting pollinators. Proper pruning helps them remain healthy and productive.

- **Renewal Pruning for Flowering and Fruiting Shrubs:** Shrubs that flower and fruit on new growth, such as elderberries, benefit greatly from renewal pruning. This technique involves cutting back old wood to ground level in late winter and thinning new stems, leaving only the 5-10 strongest canes. For elderberries specifically, heavy annual pruning encourages vigorous new growth, which results in more abundant flowers and fruit each season.
- **Shaping and Size Control:** For medicinal and culinary herbs like rosemary, sage, and lavender, pruning is essential for controlling size and promoting bushy growth. The technique involves trimming back about a third of the plant in early spring to stimulate new growth, while it's important to avoid cutting into old wood, as some herbs do not regrow from older, woody stems. For instance, with lavender, light pruning after flowering is recommended, focusing on the green stems to maintain a compact and bushy form.

5. Pruning Ground Cover Plants

Ground cover plants, like strawberries, comfrey, and creeping thyme, help prevent erosion, suppress weeds, and contribute organic matter.

- **Rejuvenation Pruning for Perennial Ground Covers:** Some ground covers, such as comfrey, benefit from periodic pruning to manage their spread and promote renewed growth. The technique involves cutting the entire plant back to ground level after flowering, which encourages fresh growth and prevents excessive spreading. For example, comfrey can be pruned 2-3 times during the growing season, allowing for the renewal of leaves that can then be used as mulch or compost.

- **Runner Removal in Strawberries:** Strawberries produce runners that can overcrowd plants and compete for nutrients, so trimming back these runners is essential to focus the plant's energy on fruit production and prevent overcrowding. In the case of June-bearing strawberries, it's important to remove runners during the first year to establish a strong root system. For established patches, runners should be trimmed as needed to manage their spread effectively.

6. Pruning Vines and Climbers

Vining plants like grapes and kiwi provide vertical layers and require annual pruning to control size and promote fruiting.

- **Spur Pruning for Grapes:** Grapes produce fruit on one-year-old wood, making annual pruning essential for maximizing yields. The technique involves cutting back fruiting canes to spurs with 2-3 buds each in late winter while removing excess growth to improve light exposure. For grapevines trained on a trellis, this means removing most of the previous year's growth and retaining only the main branches with short, fruiting spurs to promote healthy fruit production.

- **Canopy Control for Kiwi and Hardy Vines:** Kiwi vines grow vigorously and require yearly pruning to manage their size and ensure that light reaches the entire plant. The technique involves trimming back excess growth in late winter by removing tangled or weak branches and thinning crowded areas to promote good air circulation. For hardy kiwis, this means cutting back side branches to 6-10 buds, creating a structure that supports manageable and productive growth.

7. Pruning Herbs and Annuals

Herbs and some annual plants can also benefit from periodic pruning, which encourages denser growth and prolongs productivity.

- **Pinching and Cutting Back Herbs:** Herbs like basil, mint, and oregano benefit from pinching back, as this technique encourages branching and bushy growth. By regularly pinching off the tips of stems, especially before flowering, energy is redirected toward leaf development. For example, in basil, frequent pinching helps prevent flowering and promotes abundant leaf growth.
- **Cutting Back Annual Vegetables:** Some annuals, such as tomatoes and peppers, yield more fruit when pruned to remove excess foliage. The technique involves pruning suckers, or side shoots,

from the main stem to focus the plant's energy on fruit production, while being careful not to over-prune since leaves are essential for photosynthesis. For instance, with tomatoes, it's beneficial to prune side shoots below the first flower cluster, particularly for indeterminate varieties, to maintain a manageable plant structure.

Pruning techniques vary based on plant type, growth patterns, and the desired role of each plant in a food forest. Whether managing canopy trees, shrubs, ground covers, or climbers, careful pruning enhances plant health, optimizes yields, and maintains balance within the forest ecosystem. Through thoughtful pruning, food forest practitioners can promote a thriving, resilient, and productive landscape.

PEST AND DISEASE CONTROL

Controlling pests and diseases in a food forest requires a holistic approach that integrates natural pest management, biodiversity, healthy soil practices, and strategic plant selection. A food forest's diverse ecosystem offers numerous ways to mitigate pest and disease pressure without relying on synthetic chemicals, which can harm beneficial organisms and disrupt ecological balance. Below is a comprehensive guide on effective pest and disease control strategies in a food forest:

Encouraging Biodiversity to Create a Balanced Ecosystem

A diverse plant ecosystem reduces pest and disease outbreaks by attracting natural pest controllers through various planting strategies. Incorporating multiple planting layers—like canopy, understory, shrub, herbaceous, and ground cover—creates habitats that enhance biodiversity. For example, herbs and flowers like dill, yarrow, and marigold in lower layers attract predatory insects such as ladybugs and lacewings, which prey on pests like aphids and mites. Companion planting also helps, as plants like garlic and chives emit sulfur compounds that repel pests and protect nearby crops, including fruit trees, from fungal infections. Creating wildlife habitats by installing birdhouses encourages insect-eating birds like bluebirds to nest, naturally controlling caterpillar and beetle populations. Together, these strategies foster a balanced, resilient ecosystem that minimizes the need for chemical pest control.

Promoting Soil Health to Boost Plant Immunity

Healthy, nutrient-rich soil strengthens plants and makes them more resilient to pests and diseases through key practices that support soil health and biodiversity. Mulching conserves moisture, reduces weed competition, and provides habitat for beneficial soil organisms that control pathogens. For instance, applying organic mulch like straw or wood chips around fruit trees encourages beneficial fungi to outcompete harmful pathogens. Adding compost and organic matter regularly enriches the soil, increasing microbial diversity and bolstering plants' resistance to disease. Composting annually in vulnerable areas, like berry patches, helps suppress root-related fungal pathogens. Mycorrhizal fungi form symbiotic relationships with plant roots, enhancing nutrient uptake and disease resistance. Inoculating soil with these fungi when planting trees or shrubs improves root health and overall resilience. Together, these soil-enhancing strategies foster a healthy ecosystem that naturally supports plant vitality.

Using Trap Crops to Divert Pests Away from Main Crops

Trap crops are used to attract pests away from primary crops, focusing pest populations on sacrificial plants to protect more valuable crops. By choosing trap crops that appeal to specific pests and planting them strategically, pests are drawn away from main crops. For example, nasturtiums are highly attractive to aphids and can be planted around brassicas to keep aphids from reaching primary crops. Managing trap crops is essential—monitoring and removing or treating infested plants prevents pest spread. If nasturtiums become heavily infested with aphids, pruning and disposing of affected plants can help reduce the overall aphid population, thus protecting the food forest. This approach uses trap crops both as a lure and a control method, enhancing pest management naturally.

Applying Physical Barriers to Protect Vulnerable Plants

Physical barriers are an effective way to prevent pests from reaching plants, especially useful for young or vulnerable crops. **Row covers and netting** provide protection from flying insects and birds without blocking sunlight or rain. For instance, placing fine mesh netting over berries keeps birds from eating the fruit while allowing plants to thrive. **Tree guards and mulch collars** prevent damage from rodents and root-boring insects, safeguarding the roots and trunks of trees. Wrapping tree bases with tree guards deters voles and rabbits, while collars around the base protect against root borers. Together, these barriers offer targeted protection to maintain plant health and reduce pest impact.

Implementing Integrated Pest Management (IPM)

Integrated Pest Management (IPM) combines monitoring, assessment, and targeted action to control pests only when necessary, reducing reliance on broad-spectrum treatments. Regular monitoring is crucial—routinely inspecting plants for early signs of pests or diseases helps catch issues before they escalate. For example, checking leaf undersides for eggs, aphids, or fungal spots allows for prompt intervention if pest numbers increase Using biocontrols introduces beneficial organisms to target specific pests naturally; releasing parasitic wasps, for instance, helps manage caterpillar and aphid populations without chemicals. When pest levels threaten plant health, spot treatment with organic options, like insecticidal soap or neem oil, provides a targeted solution. Applying neem oil on infested leaves can control fungal infections and reduce aphid numbers. Together, these IPM strategies create a balanced approach to pest management that protects plant health sustainably.

Practicing Disease-Resistant Plant Selection

Choosing disease-resistant varieties and promoting genetic diversity are effective ways to reduce the risk of infections in a food forest. Selecting resistant varieties tailored to regional conditions minimizes the need for chemical treatments, as these plants are naturally less susceptible to specific diseases. For instance, apple varieties like 'Liberty' and 'Enterprise' resist apple scab, cutting down on potential infections. Additionally, avoiding monocultures by planting multiple varieties of the same species increases genetic diversity, which limits the spread of disease. Planting several elderberry cultivars, for example, prevents total crop loss if one variety proves susceptible. Together, these strategies create a more resilient, disease-resistant ecosystem.

Pruning and Hygiene to Prevent Disease Spread

Proper pruning and sanitation are essential for preventing the spread of fungal diseases and bacterial infections in a garden or food forest. Pruning for airflow helps reduce the high humidity in dense canopies that encourages fungal growth; for instance, open-center pruning on fruit trees like peaches and plums increases sunlight and air circulation, minimizing disease risk. Additionally, removing diseased material immediately helps contain pathogens. Disposing of leaves affected by powdery mildew, rather than composting, prevents spores from contaminating the soil. Finally, sanitizing tools regularly prevent the transfer of diseases between plants; dipping pruners in a diluted bleach solution between cuts is effective when working with infected plants. These practices work together to maintain a healthy, disease-resistant environment.

Applying Natural and Organic Sprays for Disease Control

Certain organic sprays provide effective disease prevention and management without harming beneficial organisms, making them valuable tools in sustainable gardening. Neem oil acts as a natural insecticide and fungicide, controlling a variety of pests and fungal infections; applying it on young plant foliage in early spring helps protect against powdery mildew and aphids. Baking soda solution is another simple, preventive option for fungal growth; spraying a mix of baking soda and water on vulnerable plants like cucumbers can help prevent powdery mildew. Additionally, compost tea introduces beneficial microorganisms into the soil, which can suppress harmful soil-borne diseases. For example, applying compost tea around the base of fruit trees prone to root rot allows these microbes to outcompete harmful pathogens. Together, these organic sprays offer a gentle yet effective approach to plant health management.

Practicing Crop Rotation and Polyculture

Rotating crops and planting diverse species are effective strategies for preventing soil nutrient depletion and breaking pest and disease cycles. Crop rotation avoids the buildup of soil pathogens associated with specific plant families by shifting annual crops to different areas each year. For instance repeatedly planting tomatoes in the same spot can lead to soil-borne diseases like Verticillium wilt, so rotating them reduces this risk. Polyculture planting further protects plant health by mixing species, which disrupts pest and disease spread as different plants attract various insects and pathogens. For example, a mix of root vegetables, legumes, and herbs in one area reduces pest pressure on any single type of plant. Together, these methods support soil health and resilience against pests and diseases.

Effective pest and disease control in a food forest relies on a balanced approach that combines biodiversity, healthy soil, organic treatments, and careful plant management. By fostering a diverse, resilient ecosystem and implementing these sustainable techniques, food forest practitioners can maintain plant health and productivity, reducing the need for external interventions and promoting a thriving, self-sustaining environment.

FERTILIZATION AND SOIL AMENDMENT

Fertilizing a food forest involves enriching the soil to provide nutrients for plants in a way that supports a self-sustaining ecosystem. Rather than conventional fertilizers, food forests often use natural, regenerative approaches to fertilization, emphasizing organic matter, nitrogen-fixing plants, and microbial health. Soil is the foundation of a food forest. Healthy soil contains a rich mix of organic matter, beneficial microbes, and nutrients that plants can readily absorb. Soil testing is essential to determine the pH, organic matter, and nutrient levels, helping guide which amendments and fertilization strategies will be most beneficial. For example, if the soil is acidic and low in phosphorus, applying natural amendments like bone meal or rock phosphate can help balance it. Additionally, building soil structure by incorporating organic matter such as compost, manure, or leaf litter improves soil structure, allowing for better root penetration and nutrient retention. For instance, layering 2-3 inches of compost annually on the forest floor supports nutrient cycling and retains soil moisture.

Using Mulching to Maintain Fertility

Mulching is a core technique in food forest fertilization, as organic mulch decomposes over time, providing a steady nutrient supply. Applying mulch involves using materials like wood chips, straw, leaves, or grass clippings around plants to enrich the soil as they decompose. For example, in areas with fruit trees, applying wood chips or a mix of fallen leaves and grass clippings around the base improves the soil, suppresses weeds, and maintains moisture. Moreover, mimicking natural forest layers can be beneficial; by allowing fallen leaves to stay on the forest floor, a self-feeding system is created where nutrients are continually recycled. For instance, letting leaves from canopy trees fall around understory plants allows them to naturally decompose and provide nutrients.

Incorporating Nitrogen-Fixing Plants for Sustainable Fertility

Nitrogen-fixing plants are a natural way to enrich the soil with nitrogen, an essential nutrient for plant growth, as they form symbiotic relationships with bacteria in their roots that convert atmospheric nitrogen into a form plants can use. **Planting nitrogen-fixers** involves integrating legumes and nitrogen-fixing shrubs and trees, such as clover, alders, and peas, within the food forest. For example, planting clover around fruit trees provides ground cover and fixes nitrogen into the soil, benefiting nearby plants. Additionally, the **chop-and-drop** technique involves cutting nitrogen-fixing plants periodically and allowing them to decompose in place, adding nutrients directly to the soil. An example of this is pruning back leguminous shrubs like Siberian pea shrub or autumn olive and letting the cuttings decompose on-site to feed the soil.

Using Compost and Organic Matter for Ongoing Fertility

Compost is a rich, well-rounded fertilizer that adds essential nutrients and supports soil microorganisms. Applying compost involves spreading it around the base of plants or creating compost pits throughout the food forest to distribute nutrients evenly. For instance, applying a thin layer of compost in early spring around berry bushes and herbs benefits them with a fresh nutrient boost at the start of the growing season. Moreover, composting organic waste on-site allows for the recycling of organic waste, such as vegetable scraps, weeds, and leaves, into nutrient-rich material. An example of this is creating a composting area near the vegetable garden section of the forest for convenience and nutrient cycling.

Implementing Green Manures and Cover Crops

Green manures and cover crops improve soil fertility and structure by covering bare soil, adding organic matter, and fixing nitrogen. Choosing cover crops involves selecting varieties like winter rye, vetch, and clover that fit the food forest's needs based on seasonal cycles. For example, planting a mix of clover and vetch between rows of fruit trees in late fall protects the soil over winter and enriches it in spring. Furthermore, turning in green manure at the end of the cover crop cycle entails cutting down the plants and either turning them into the soil or leaving them as surface mulch. An example of this practice is chopping down a winter cover crop of rye in spring and incorporating it into the soil to add nitrogen and organic matter.

Utilizing Animal Integration for Fertility

Animals can play a vital role in fertilizing a food forest by recycling nutrients back into the soil. Managed grazing involves using animals like chickens, ducks, or goats for light grazing to naturally fertilize the forest with manure. For example, allowing chickens to roam in specific areas of the food forest enables them to eat pests, scratch the soil, and deposit nutrient-rich droppings. Composting animal manure is essential before applying it to plants to avoid nitrogen burn and reduce pathogen risks. An example of this practice is aging chicken or rabbit manure in a compost pile for several months before spreading it around fruiting plants.

Applying Natural Fertilizers and Soil Amendments

Specific organic fertilizers and soil amendments can help address nutrient deficiencies without disturbing the ecosystem balance. Rock phosphate provides phosphorus, which encourages strong root growth and flowering.

For instance, if soil tests show low phosphorus, adding rock phosphate around berry plants or grapevines in the fall can improve fruiting. Kelp meal and seaweed contain trace minerals and stimulate microbial activity in the soil. An example of using this is applying a thin layer of kelp meal around herbaceous plants in spring for an extra boost of trace nutrients. Moreover, bone meal and blood meal supply nitrogen and phosphorus, which are essential for leafy growth and root development. For example, adding a small amount of bone meal to the planting holes of fruit trees and shrubs supports long-term growth.

Promoting Fungal Health to Aid Nutrient Cycling

Fungi, particularly mycorrhizal fungi, play an essential role in nutrient uptake and soil health within a food forest. Inoculating soil with mycorrhizae involves introducing mycorrhizal fungi to the root zones of trees and shrubs, helping them access nutrients more effectively. For instance, using mycorrhizal inoculant when planting young trees enhances their growth and resilience through this symbiotic relationship. Additionally, maintaining moisture for fungi is crucial, as fungal growth thrives in moisture-rich environments; therefore, maintaining mulch layers ensures fungi have the conditions to flourish. An example of this practice is regularly adding wood chip mulch around larger plants to feed the fungal layer and aid nutrient transfer from soil to plant roots.

Timing and Seasonal Application of Fertilizers

The timing of fertilizer applications is important for maximizing nutrient uptake while minimizing waste. Spring fertilization should focus on nitrogen-rich materials, such as compost or green manure, in early spring when plants are emerging from dormancy and require nutrients for leaf and stem growth. For example, spreading compost around fruit trees and berry bushes in early spring supports new growth. In contrast, summer and fall nutrients should consist of phosphorus- and potassium-rich amendments applied during these seasons to promote flowering and fruiting, supporting plants as they store energy for winter. An example of this practice is top-dressing with bone meal or kelp meal around perennials like rhubarb or asparagus in late summer to enhance root and flower development for the following season.

Monitoring and Adjusting Fertilization Practices

Continually monitoring plant health, soil condition, and growth patterns is essential to assess whether the fertilization practices are effective or need adjustment. Observing plant health involves looking for signs of nutrient deficiencies, such as yellowing leaves (indicating nitrogen deficiency) or poor flowering (suggesting phosphorus deficiency), to guide future fertilization needs. For instance, if fruit trees show chlorosis (yellowing of leaves), it may be necessary to increase the organic matter and adjust pH with lime or sulfur as needed. Additionally, adjusting based on soil tests should be performed every 2-3 years to track nutrient changes and adjust fertilization methods accordingly. For example, if potassium levels drop, consider adding wood ash or composted banana peels as a natural potassium source.

Fertilizing a food forest is a cyclical, adaptive process that focuses on enriching the soil with organic matter, promoting microbial and fungal health, and utilizing natural sources of nutrients. By employing these regenerative fertilization techniques, food forest practitioners can cultivate a resilient, self-sustaining ecosystem that nurtures diverse plant life and produces abundant yields over the long term.

SOIL AMENDMENT

Soil amendment in a food forest is a crucial practice that enhances soil health, improves fertility, and supports the diverse plant life integral to this ecosystem. Effective soil amendment involves adding various organic materials and minerals to the soil to improve its structure, nutrient content, and overall biological activity, fostering a vibrant environment for plants, beneficial microbes, and soil organisms. Before implementing any amendments, it is essential to understand the current condition of the soil through soil testing, which assesses pH levels, nutrient availability, organic matter content, and microbial activity. This allows for targeted amendments that address specific deficiencies.

Soil amendments can be broadly categorized into organic and inorganic materials. Common organic matter options include compost, which enhances soil structure and provides nutrients while boosting microbial populations, aged manure from herbivores, which can improve soil fertility, leaf litter that contributes organic matter, and green manures or cover crops that increase organic matter and nitrogen levels. Mineral amendments provide essential nutrients that may be lacking in the soil, such as rock phosphate for phosphorus, greensand for potassium, and gypsum to improve soil structure. Proper application techniques include top-dressing with compost or well-rotted manure on the soil surface, incorporating mineral amendments into the top 6-12 inches of soil, or building raised beds with a rich mix of compost and organic matter to improve drainage and nutrient content. The timing of soil amendments is also critical; applying compost and organic matter in early spring provides nutrients during the peak growing season, while fall application allows organic matter to decompose over the winter.

After amendments are applied, continuous monitoring is essential to ensure soil health remains optimal through regular soil testing every few years to track nutrient levels and pH changes, as well as observing plant health for signs of nutrient deficiency. Integrating soil health practices with other management techniques, such as mulching to conserve moisture and suppress weeds, diversifying plant species to encourage different root structures, and attracting beneficial organisms like earthworms and mycorrhizal fungi, contributes to a balanced ecosystem. In conclusion, soil amendment in a food forest is an ongoing process that requires observation, understanding, and adaptation; by employing various organic and mineral amendments, monitoring soil health, and integrating practices that foster biodiversity, a food forest can thrive, producing healthy plants while enhancing soil structure and fertility for future generations, ultimately creating a self-sustaining ecosystem where soil health underpins plant vitality, resulting in a resilient and productive food forest.

WATER MANAGEMENT

Water management in a food forest is essential for creating a resilient and self-sustaining ecosystem, as proper water management supports plant growth, minimizes erosion, prevents drought stress, and promotes soil health. A comprehensive guide to water management techniques in a food forest begins with understanding site hydrology. The first step in managing water is to analyze the landscape's natural water flow, which informs decisions on planting, mulching, and irrigation. This involves observing where water flows, pools, and drains after rainfall.

Assessing natural water flow is crucial; identifying slopes, valleys, and flat areas helps determine where water naturally accumulates or drains. For example, in a sloped area, water will move downhill, so it is advisable to plant drought-tolerant plants higher on the slopes while placing water-loving species at the base where water collects. Additionally, mapping soil type and drainage is essential, as different soil types hold or drain water at varying rates. Clay retains water, while sandy soil drains quickly. Conducting soil tests helps determine which amendments, like adding organic matter, can improve water retention or drainage. For instance, in sandy soils, adding compost and mulch will help retain moisture, whereas clay soils may benefit from raised beds or swales to prevent waterlogging.

Another effective technique for water management is mulching, which is one of the simplest ways to conserve moisture in a food forest. Mulch insulates the soil, prevents evaporation, and promotes the growth of beneficial soil microbes. Applying organic mulch involves using materials like wood chips, straw, leaves, or compost around trees, shrubs, and plants. This organic matter decomposes over time, adding nutrients to the soil while improving water retention. For example, mulching around fruit trees with wood chips or straw can reduce the frequency of watering by retaining soil moisture and minimizing competition from weeds.

Layering mulch appropriately is also important for water management; applying mulch in layers of 2-4 inches is recommended, as thicker layers may lead to water pooling or fungal growth on the surface. An example of effective layering would be applying a 3-inch layer of straw mulch around vegetable beds to maintain consistent soil moisture, which is particularly beneficial for shallow-rooted plants. Overall, understanding site hydrology and utilizing effective mulching techniques are fundamental components of water management in a food forest, leading to improved plant health and a thriving ecosystem.

Incorporating swales for passive water retention is an effective strategy in a food forest, as swales are shallow, level ditches built along contour lines that capture rainwater and allow it to slowly infiltrate into the soil, thereby reducing runoff and erosion. The design of swales is crucial; they should be dug along the contour of a slope and filled with organic material, such as wood chips or logs, which slows water movement and allows more to sink into the soil. For example, on a hillside, a series of swales spaced 10-15 feet apart can capture runoff during heavy rains, helping to irrigate trees and plants along the slope.

Using swales in conjunction with planting enhances water management. Planting water-loving species along the lower side of swales, where moisture is abundant, helps maintain a diversity of plant species within a food forest. For instance, planting elderberries or willows near swales will allow these plants to benefit from the additional moisture, as they naturally thrive in wetter conditions. Overall, the incorporation of swales not only facilitates passive water retention but also promotes plant diversity and health in a food forest ecosystem.

Preparation of Hugelkultur for Moisture Retention and Soil Building

Creating a hugelkultur bed involves layering organic material, such as logs and branches, to create a raised bed that retains moisture and builds soil fertility over time. Hugelkultur is particularly useful in food forests, as it improves water retention, enhances soil health, and requires minimal maintenance once established. To prepare a hugelkultur bed for moisture retention and soil building, follow these steps:

First, select a suitable site based on the needs of the plants you plan to grow, as well as the natural landscape and water flow of your food forest. Consider the sunlight requirements of the plants you'll grow on the bed, selecting a sunny spot for sun-loving crops or a partially shaded area for shade-tolerant plants. Additionally, place the bed in an area where it can intercept water flow or capture runoff, especially in arid environments. Next, plan the bed size and shape based on available materials and the space in your food forest. Hugelkultur beds are typically 3-5 feet high to maximize moisture retention and soil depth, though they can be built shorter if needed. The width can vary, but a 4-6 feet width provides a good balance for planting and maintenance. Design the bed in a shape that suits your landscape—straight, curved, or mounded, depending on aesthetic and functional goals.

Hugelkultur bed

Then, gather the materials needed to construct the bed. Hugelkultur beds are built using a range of organic materials that break down over time to improve soil fertility and water-holding capacity. Start with a base layer of large logs, branches, and tree trunks, as these retain moisture while decomposing and serve as a reservoir for the bed. Use hardwoods like oak, maple, or alder for longevity, and avoid wood from trees containing allelopathic chemicals, such as black walnut, which can inhibit plant growth. For the intermediate layer, incorporate finer branches, twigs, and smaller pieces of wood to help fill gaps and create a more stable structure. Include nitrogen-rich materials, such as green leaves, manure, or grass clippings, to offset the carbon-heavy wood base; these will aid in initial decomposition and prevent nitrogen depletion in the soil. Finally, add a top layer composed of a mixture of soil and compost to provide a suitable planting medium for seeds and young plants.

To build a hugelkultur bed effectively, start by clearing the ground where you plan to construct it. Remove any vegetation or rocks, and consider digging a shallow trench to provide stability and define the bed's base. In dry climates, trenching can be beneficial; dig a trench 6-12 inches deep to create a sunken base that will retain more water, while in wetter climates, trenching may not be necessary. Next, lay the base layer of logs and large wood. Place the largest logs and wood pieces in the trench or on the ground, arranging them to form a stable base. The wood will absorb water and slowly decompose over time, providing moisture and nutrients. For optimal placement, stack the logs lengthwise along the bed's base to ensure stability, but avoid piling them too high at this stage to prevent instability.

After securing the large logs, proceed to add smaller branches and twigs. Fill in the gaps between the larger logs with these smaller pieces, as this layer adds structure, fills voids, and allows for better air circulation within the mound. Use a layering technique by spreading the smaller branches evenly over the logs, ensuring they cover all areas to create a dense and stable foundation. In Order to balance the high-carbon wood, incorporate a layer of nitrogen-rich materials, such as green leaves, grass clippings, manure, or kitchen scraps. This layer will help accelerate decomposition and prevent the wood from pulling nitrogen out of the soil. Spread the nitrogen-rich material evenly across the mound to ensure that decomposition occurs uniformly, supporting the overall health and productivity of the hugelkultur bed.

To create a successful hugelkultur bed, begin by layering a thick mixture of soil and compost on top of the previously placed wood and green material layers. This layer will serve as the primary planting surface, providing essential nutrients and structure for plant roots. Ensure the layer is at least 6-12 inches thick, as this allows for proper root growth and helps retain moisture at the top of the bed, while also confirming that the soil is well-draining yet capable of holding enough moisture for the plants you plan to grow. Next, shape and tamp down the bed using a rake or shovel, creating a rounded or sloped top to facilitate water distribution and stability. While shaping, gently tamp down the layers to prevent excessive settling, but press lightly to maintain some air space, which is necessary for root growth and microbial activity.

After shaping the bed, thoroughly water the hugelkultur bed. This initial deep watering helps settle the materials and kickstarts the decomposition process. Ensure the entire bed, particularly the wood at the core, is well-moistened, as this will aid decomposition and enhance the bed's initial moisture retention capacity. Once the bed is constructed and watered, you can begin planting. Choose plants based on their water and nutrient needs, taking into account the bed's moisture gradient, with wetter conditions near the base and drier conditions near the top. For example, place moisture-loving crops like strawberries or squash near the bottom, where water retention is highest, while drought-tolerant plants like thyme and rosemary are better suited for the top.

For added benefits, you may apply a final layer of mulch, using materials such as straw, wood chips, or leaves on top of the soil. This mulch layer helps retain moisture, reduces erosion, and further prevents weed growth. Aim for a mulch depth of 2-3 inches, ensuring you do not cover the stems of young plants directly to avoid rotting. Over time, as the wood decomposes and the soil structure changes, it is crucial to maintain and monitor the bed. Regularly check to ensure the bed stays moist, and replenish mulch and compost as needed. Each growing season, top up the soil and compost layer to replace nutrients and improve soil structure, and be sure to water the bed as necessary, especially during dry spells, to maintain the decomposition process and keep the plants healthy.

Hugelkultur beds offer numerous benefits, including water conservation and support for rich microbial activity, which enhances soil fertility and plant growth over time. They promote biodiversity by creating varied moisture and nutrient zones, making them ideal for a diverse range of plant species in a food forest. This method leverages natural decomposition, making it a sustainable and cost-effective strategy for building soil and retaining moisture, particularly in low-rainfall regions.

Rainwater Harvesting for Supplemental Irrigation

Rainwater harvesting systems, such as rain barrels or cisterns, collect and store rainwater from gutters to provide a renewable water source, especially useful during dry periods. This reduces dependence on municipal or well water by enabling the storage and later distribution of rainwater to critical areas, such as young trees and vegetables that require extra moisture for establishment. Gravity-fed irrigation systems, like hoses or drip lines, can channel this stored rainwater to various parts of a food forest. By using gravity, water flows efficiently without energy input, allowing precise watering for herbaceous plants in guilds around fruit trees, ensuring optimal water distribution with minimal effort.

Designing Tree and Plant Placement for Water Efficiency

Strategic plant placement involves grouping species based on their water needs to reduce waste and ensure efficient irrigation. This approach, known as water zoning, positions water-loving plants, such as mint and comfrey, closer to swales or rain catchment areas, while drought-tolerant plants like rosemary and sage are placed in drier zones. Additionally, taller canopy trees provide shade, helping to conserve moisture by creating a cooler microclimate below. This allows shade-loving understory plants, like ferns or ginger, to thrive beneath the canopy, benefiting from reduced sunlight and retained soil moisture.

Greywater Systems for Sustainable Irrigation

Greywater systems recycle water from household sources like sinks and showers, providing a sustainable irrigation method for a food forest, particularly beneficial in dry climates. By installing a greywater diverter on household plumbing, water can be routed to the forest, but it's essential that this water is free of harsh chemicals. This recycled water is ideal for low-maintenance shrubs or trees, such as figs and elderberries, that can tolerate occasional greywater. To further enhance distribution and prevent clogging, mulch basins or filters can be added to greywater outlets, creating a slow-spreading infiltration basin near fruit trees. This setup allows water to reach the root zone without pooling, promoting efficient and sustainable irrigation.

Implementing Drip Irrigation and Low-Flow Systems

Drip irrigation and soaker hoses deliver water directly to plant root zones, reducing evaporation and runoff. Drip lines can be installed at the base of each plant, customized to meet individual water needs, and connected to rain barrels for efficiency. For example, using drip irrigation around berry patches ensures consistent moisture, which is crucial for fruit production during dry spells. Low-flow emitters provide slow, deep irrigation, which minimizes water waste. This setup is ideal for young trees that need steady watering in their initial years, helping establish strong root systems with minimal water loss.

Using Ground Cover Plants to Retain Soil Moisture

Ground cover plants help reduce soil evaporation, control erosion, and enhance soil fertility as they decompose. Selecting fast-spreading ground covers, like clover, creeping thyme, or vetch, prevents weed growth and conserves moisture. For instance, planting creeping clover around fruit trees acts as a living mulch, retaining moisture and contributing nitrogen to the soil as it breaks down. Ground covers also serve as living mulch around larger plants, retaining moisture and enriching the soil. In strawberry beds, interplanting with white clover preserves soil moisture and improves soil health without competing with strawberries for water.

Monitoring and Adjusting Water Management Practices

Regularly assessing water needs, soil moisture, and plant health allows for ongoing improvement of water management strategies. Observing plant health can reveal signs of water stress, such as wilting, poor growth, or discoloration, indicating adjustments may be needed. For instance, if young trees display drought stress, increasing mulch thickness or adjusting irrigation can improve water availability. Moisture sensors can also be installed to monitor soil moisture, particularly in high-demand or poorly drained areas. Placing sensors around vegetable beds, for example, helps determine when watering is actually required, preventing unnecessary irrigation and conserving water.

Effective water management in a food forest integrates natural techniques, such as mulching, swales, and appropriate plant placement, with sustainable irrigation solutions like rainwater harvesting and greywater use. By mimicking natural ecosystems and tailoring water practices to site-specific conditions, a food forest can conserve water, maintain healthy plant growth, and thrive as a resilient, self-sustaining system. This approach not only benefits the plants but also supports a diverse ecosystem that can withstand environmental changes and seasonal droughts.

ATTRACTING BENEFICIAL INSECTS

Attracting beneficial insects is a fundamental aspect of maintaining a healthy, resilient food forest. These insects play critical roles in pollination, natural pest control, and overall ecosystem balance. From ladybugs to predatory thrips, fostering an environment that supports a diverse array of beneficial insects can significantly enhance the productivity and sustainability of your food forest. This comprehensive guide explores the process of attracting beneficial insects, detailing strategies, plant selections, habitat enhancements, and best practices to create a thriving ecosystem.

Beneficial insects play multiple vital roles in a food forest ecosystem, contributing to its productivity, health, and resilience. Pollinators such as bees, butterflies, and certain beetles facilitate the pollination of fruiting plants, leading to improved fruit set and yield. Predatory and parasitic insects, including ladybugs, lacewings, and predatory thrips, provide natural pest control by feeding on herbivorous pests, helping to maintain balance without the need for chemical interventions. Additionally, certain insects enhance soil health through aeration and decomposition, which improves soil fertility and structure.

Attracting beneficial insects to a food forest requires thoughtful strategies that integrate a variety of plantings, habitats, and maintenance practices. Pollen and nectar plants like dill, fennel, and coriander provide essential food sources, while creating varied plant heights and structures ensures diverse habitats for beneficial insects. Minimal disturbance, such as avoiding excessive pruning, helps maintain undisturbed environments. Hoverflies, for instance, are drawn to rich floral sources and benefit from moist areas that support their larvae. Supporting beneficial insects also involves promoting plant diversity, as a mix of flowering annuals, perennials, and biennials—such as calendula, borage, cosmos, lavender, and sunflowers—provides continuous nectar and pollen throughout the growing season. Aromatic herbs like dill, fennel, basil, and mint further attract insects while repelling pests.

Providing habitat and shelter is crucial; windbreaks, shelterbelts, mulch layers, leaf litter, insect hotels, and shallow water sources with pebbles offer protection, nesting sites, and drinking water. Companion planting complements these efforts, as pairing certain plants enhances pest control and plant health—for example, marigolds near vegetables repel nematodes, and basil alongside tomatoes deters whiteflies and enriches tomato flavor. To protect these beneficial populations, minimizing pesticide use is essential. Organic pest control, such as neem oil and insecticidal soaps, along with Integrated Pest Management (IPM), ensures pests are managed in a way that avoids harming helpful insects.

Maintaining continuous bloom ensures food for beneficial insects throughout the season, with early bloomers like crocuses and late bloomers like asters providing nectar and pollen across the year. Succession planting, or staggering flower plantings, keeps food sources steady. Encouraging natural predators, such as insect-eating birds and bats, is another key step; installing birdhouses and bat houses brings in allies that consume large quantities of pests. Together, these strategies foster a balanced and resilient food forest ecosystem that supports a wide range of beneficial insects, enhances pest control, promotes pollination, and strengthens biodiversity.

Creating favorable environmental conditions and integrating beneficial insect support are essential strategies for a thriving food forest ecosystem. Optimizing microclimates by providing ample sunlight for sun-loving insects like bees and shaded areas for species like parasitic wasps helps ensure a balanced environment. Trees and shrubs can regulate temperature, shielding beneficial insects from extreme conditions.

Providing nesting sites, such as bee hotels or bare soil for ground-nesting bees, as well as planting host plants for butterfly larval development, further supports insect life cycles. Maintaining plant health through proper watering, fertilization, pruning, and weeding keeps plants resilient to pests and reduces the need for pest control measures that might harm beneficial insects.

Integrating beneficial insect support into food forest management involves regular monitoring and adaptive strategies. Observing and identifying beneficial insects, tracking pest populations, and assessing insect abundance guide decisions on planting adjustments, introducing new species or removing plants that attract pests. Community engagement through education and collaboration with local gardens extends these practices, creating wider networks of beneficial insect habitats. Practical examples, like an integrated orchard guild with apple trees, chives, nasturtiums, and clover, demonstrate how specific plant combinations repel aphids, enrich soil, and improve pollination, while herbaceous borders and swale planting enhance pest control and water retention.

Challenges, such as attracting sufficient beneficial insects, balancing pest control with plantings, and managing invasive species, require thoughtful solutions. Increasing plant diversity, combining pest control strategies, and replacing invasive plants with native, insect-friendly species help address these obstacles. Best practices include promoting plant diversity, ensuring continuous nectar and pollen availability through staggered blooming, providing habitat and nesting resources, minimizing chemical use, and adapting management based on observations. A holistic approach to attracting and maintaining beneficial insects, supported by practices like companion planting and organic pest control, reduces reliance on chemicals and enhances the resilience and productivity of the food forest. By fostering a balanced ecosystem, beneficial insects like ladybugs and predatory thrips naturally manage pests and aid pollination, contributing to the overall health and sustainability of the food forest.

KEY BENEFICIAL INSECTS TO ATTRACT
Ladybugs (Ladybird Beetles)

To attract ladybugs to your garden or food forest and benefit from their natural pest control, it's essential to create a welcoming environment with suitable plants, food sources, shelter, and favorable conditions that encourage them to settle in. Ladybugs, known for feeding on pests like aphids, mites, and whiteflies, support pest control and ecosystem health. Start by planting ladybug-friendly flowers and herbs, such as umbelliferous flowers (like dill, fennel, cilantro, yarrow, and Queen Anne's lace) and composites like daisies, cosmos, marigolds, and sunflowers, which offer easy nectar sources. Fragrant herbs like mint, lavender, oregano, thyme, and basil, as well as cover crops like clover and alfalfa, also attract ladybugs and provide shelter.

To encourage ladybugs, provide food sources beyond nectar and pollen. Ladybugs feed on soft-bodied insects, especially aphids, so planting "sacrificial" or "trap" plants like nasturtiums or marigolds in low-risk areas attracts aphids and subsequently draws ladybugs. Varied habitats also support prey like mealybugs, mites, thrips, and insect eggs, providing a rich food chain for ladybugs. Creating shelter is crucial, as ladybugs need places to hide, reproduce, and hibernate. Dense ground covers like clover, thyme, or alyssum offer shaded, sheltered spots, while leaving leaf litter and mulch retains moisture and provides cover. Insect hotels or DIY ladybug shelters with hollow reeds or bamboo near ground cover plants can create cozy overwintering spots.

Ladybug attacking an aphid
A water source is essential for ladybugs, particularly in hot weather. Provide a shallow dish filled with clean water and pebbles so ladybugs can safely drink, or mist plants regularly to create moisture without stagnant

water that could attract mosquitoes. To support ladybugs long-term, limit or avoid pesticides, which kill beneficial insects and reduce their food. Opt for organic pest control, like neem oil or insecticidal soap, applied selectively, and focus on maintaining a diverse, pesticide-free ecosystem with varied flowering plants, perennial ground covers, and patches of continuously blooming plants to encourage not only ladybugs but other beneficial insects.

Lady beetle larva attacks an aphid

While buying ladybugs for release is possible, it's typically more effective to attract native ladybugs that are adapted to your climate. If you do release purchased ladybugs, release them at dusk to reduce their tendency to fly away, mist nearby plants with water, and place them near aphid-infested plants for an immediate food source. Attracting ladybugs naturally supports a balanced, pest-resistant food forest or garden over the long term, fostering an ecosystem where ladybugs thrive and contribute to the overall health of your garden.

Predatory Thrips
Predatory Thrips

Predatory thrips are small, beneficial insects vital for natural pest control, feeding on harmful pests like mites, whiteflies, aphids, and the larval stages of some other thrips species. Unlike their plant-eating relatives, these predatory thrips actively consume pests, supporting sustainable pest management and reducing the need for chemical interventions. To attract them to a food forest or garden, start by understanding their role and the types of pests they target, such as spider mites, whiteflies, aphids, and plant-damaging thrips species, which helps prevent pest outbreaks that could harm crops.

Planting a diverse selection of flowers provides predatory thrips with necessary pollen and nectar, especially when pest populations are low. Plants in the Asteraceae family, like daisies, cosmos, marigolds, sunflowers, and asters, offer accessible nectar sources, while umbelliferous plants from the Apiaceae family, such as dill, fennel, yarrow, and cilantro, have dense clusters of flowers that attract various beneficial insects. Small flowering herbs like thyme, oregano, chamomile, and coriander further add diversity and support thrips through continuous blooms across the growing season. Providing suitable habitats, such as ground cover and organic mulch, creates a stable environment for predatory thrips to shelter and reproduce. Mulches like straw, leaves, or wood chips improve soil health, retain moisture, and foster a cooler microhabitat preferred by these insects. Low-growing ground covers, like clover and creeping thyme, add shelter and attract other insects that predatory thrips may feed on, supporting a healthy balance in the ecosystem.

Minimizing or avoiding pesticide use is crucial, as chemical pesticides can harm predatory thrips and other beneficial insects. Instead, choose targeted organic solutions, like insecticidal soap or neem oil, when necessary, and apply them to specific areas rather than broadly. This practice allows predatory thrips to thrive and maintain natural pest control. Predatory thrips also need water, so providing a shallow dish with pebbles or misting plants regularly offers moisture without attracting pests. This water source is particularly beneficial in dry climates or during droughts, helping predatory thrips survive and remain active in pest management. Encouraging a diverse insect ecosystem further enhances the effectiveness of predatory thrips. Attracting other beneficial insects, like ladybugs, lacewings, and spiders, creates a balanced habitat where various predators work together in pest control. This diversity builds resilience and allows predatory thrips to function effectively within the ecosystem.

Lacewings

Attracting lacewings to your garden or food forest offers a sustainable way to control pests naturally. Lacewings, especially in their larval stage, are powerful predators of harmful pests like aphids, whiteflies, and mealybugs. By creating an environment that supports lacewings' needs for food, shelter, and water, gardeners can leverage their pest control abilities while reducing the need for chemical pesticides. Understanding lacewing behavior is essential: adult lacewings feed on pollen, nectar, and honeydew, while the larvae prey on soft-bodied pests. To attract them, select a variety of flowers that provide nectar and pollen throughout the growing season. Plants in the Asteraceae family, such as coreopsis, cosmos, and sunflowers, offer accessible nectar, while umbelliferous plants like dill and fennel, and leguminous plants like clover, enhance overall garden health. This ensures lacewings have a continuous food supply when pest populations are low.

Including plants that attract a small number of aphids, such as broad beans, nasturtiums, or milkweed, creates a source of honeydew for adult lacewings and food for larvae. Maintaining these plants in controlled numbers fosters a balanced ecosystem without overwhelming pest populations Providing sheltered spots is another way to encourage lacewings to stay and reproduce. Lacewing houses made from straw, bamboo, or cardboard create ideal resting places, as do organic shelters like straw mulch, leaf piles, and dense ground covers like clover. These sheltered areas help lacewings find refuge and lay eggs, supporting a stable population in the garden. To protect lacewings, minimize pesticide use, as these insects are highly sensitive to broad-spectrum chemicals that can disrupt their lifecycle. Use targeted organic options like neem oil when necessary, applying them sparingly to maintain a healthy balance of pests and predators.

An ecosystem with diverse beneficial insects—such as ladybugs, parasitic wasps, and lacewings—creates a natural pest control network. Plant diversity and native wildflower mixes attract these insect allies, supporting each other's roles in managing pest populations. Lastly, providing a reliable water source keeps lacewings active, especially in dry conditions. Shallow dishes with pebbles or misting plants regularly provide safe, accessible water. By fostering a lacewing-friendly habitat with ample food sources, shelter, and minimal pesticides, you create a thriving environment where lacewings can naturally manage pests. This approach not only reduces chemical interventions but also supports a resilient, balanced ecosystem in your food forest or garden.

Green Lacewings

Parasitic Wasps

To attract parasitic wasps to your food forest, focus on enhancing the habitat with specific plants, natural habitats, and sustainable practices. Parasitic wasps, which naturally target pests like aphids, caterpillars, and beetle larvae, contribute significantly to pest control without pesticides. Here's how to create an inviting environment for these beneficial insects: First, incorporate small, nectar-rich flowers that parasitic wasps prefer, especially those with shallow nectaries for easy nectar access. Choose plants with tiny, clustered flowers that bloom throughout the year to provide a consistent nectar source. Examples include cilantro and dill, whose small, accessible blooms attract parasitic wasps, and alyssum and sweet fennel, which produce dense clusters of tiny flowers that offer nectar without attracting larger insects that may compete with parasitic wasps.

Second, use perennials to create long-term shelter that supports parasitic wasps by providing stable habitats for nesting and overwintering. Perennials reduce the need for tilling, which can disturb soil and harm these delicate insects. Consider shrubs and bushes for shelter, as they are less likely to be disturbed, and clump-forming perennials like goldenrod, yarrow, and lavender, which offer dense, wind-protected areas safe from predators. Third, reduce artificial light at night, as it disrupts the natural patterns of many beneficial wasps and increases their vulnerability to predators. By limiting artificial lighting around your food forest, you create a safer nighttime environment not only for parasitic wasps but also for other nocturnal beneficial insects. Fourth, preserve leaf litter and natural debris as overwintering sites for parasitic wasps. Rather than completely clearing out fallen leaves and branches, leave some undisturbed patches. This practice creates a microhabitat rich in fungi and decomposers, indirectly supporting a diverse ecosystem that attracts parasitic wasps.

Fifth, introduce "banker" plants for continuous food sources. These plants host pest species in a controlled way, providing a steady food source for parasitic wasps. By allowing a few sacrificial plants to attract pests like aphids or whiteflies, you support a continuous presence of parasitic wasps while keeping pest populations manageable. Also, maintain a diverse, layered planting structure to mimic natural ecosystems that parasitic wasps favor. Layered vegetation—canopy trees, understory shrubs, ground covers, and low-growing herbs—provides complex habitats that support parasitic wasps, giving them shelter from extreme temperatures.

Parasitic wasp

Specific Plant Selections to Attract Beneficial Insects

To create a balanced ecosystem that attracts beneficial insects for natural pest control, integrate specific plants in your food forest that cater to the needs of various helpful insects, including ladybugs, predatory thrips, lacewings, parasitic wasps, and hoverflies. Ladybugs, known for their aphid control, are drawn to plants like dill, which provides nectar for adults, yarrow, which attracts both ladybugs and other predatory insects, and fennel, which offers both nectar and shelter. Predatory thrips, which feed on pests like spider mites and aphids, are particularly attracted to sweet alyssum, a plant that draws in various beneficial insects, cosmos, which provides necessary nectar and pollen, and sunflowers, which serve as a hub for predatory thrips and other beneficials. Lacewings, known for pollination and aphid control, are enticed by goldenrod, which draws adult lacewings, stevia, which offers a rich supply of nectar and pollen, and nasturtiums, which serve both as a nectar source and a trap crop for pests. Parasitic wasps, essential for controlling pest larvae, are naturally drawn to plants like coriander, or cilantro, which attracts species like Encarsia formosa, borage, which supports wasp populations with nectar and pollen, and anise hyssop, which attracts a variety of parasitic wasps. Hoverflies, which aid in both pollination and pest control, are attracted to lavender, a strong nectar source, chives, which provide both nectar and shelter, and cosmos, known for its continuous blooming, supporting hoverflies throughout the growing season.

CHAPTER SEVEN

FOREST SUCCESSION

Natural succession in a food forest refers to the gradual, ecological development and transformation of the plant and animal communities within the forest over time, moving from simpler plant communities to increasingly complex ones. This process follows a predictable pattern, beginning with bare soil or a disturbed area and advancing to a stable, diverse ecosystem, known as the "climax community." Understanding and harnessing natural succession is key to designing, managing, and sustaining a productive food forest.

THE BASICS OF ECOLOGICAL SUCCESSION

Ecological succession is a fundamental process that describes how ecosystems evolve over time, beginning with the colonization of bare or disturbed land by species that gradually alter the environment, paving the way for more complex and competitive species. This dynamic progression, which can span decades or even centuries, reflects nature's way of creating balance and resilience within an ecosystem. Understanding succession helps us appreciate the intricate relationships between soil, plants, and animals, and informs sustainable practices in ecosystem restoration and agricultural methods like food forestry, where a thriving, self-sustaining system is the goal.

The two main types of ecological succession are primary and secondary succession, each marked by the initial state of the land. Primary succession occurs in places where no soil exists, such as after a volcanic eruption or glacial retreat, leaving only bare rock or mineral deposits. In these conditions, the process begins with pioneer species, which are hardy organisms capable of surviving extreme conditions and initiating soil development. Lichens and mosses are examples of pioneer species in primary succession; they can cling to rock surfaces, break down minerals, and create organic material as they grow, die, and decompose. This slow accumulation of organic matter starts forming a thin layer of soil, which allows other plants, like grasses and small herbs, to establish themselves. Over time, as more plants contribute organic material and as microorganisms and insects begin to inhabit the soil, it gradually deepens and improves in fertility. The enriched soil eventually supports shrubs, trees, and a more diverse ecosystem of animals, culminating in a stable, mature community, often referred to as a climax community. This entire process can take thousands of years, with each successive stage creating the conditions necessary for the next.

Secondary succession, on the other hand, takes place in areas where a disturbance has altered an existing ecosystem but left the soil intact. Examples include abandoned fields, areas cleared by fire, or land impacted by a windstorm. Because soil remains and often contains seeds, nutrients, and microorganisms from previous plant and animal life, secondary succession proceeds much more rapidly than primary succession. In the initial stages of secondary succession, fast-growing plants such as grasses, annuals, and herbaceous plants quickly colonize the area, taking advantage of the exposed nutrients and sunlight. These early colonizers stabilize the soil, reduce erosion, and create microhabitats that allow other species to grow. As these plants mature, they improve soil conditions by adding organic matter and nitrogen, encouraging more complex plant species, such as shrubs and pioneer trees, to establish themselves. Over time, the landscape transitions to support larger, long-lived trees, and eventually a diverse, multi-layered forest develops, full of species interactions and ecological roles.

In the context of a food forest, secondary succession is particularly relevant, as many food forests are established on previously cultivated or disturbed land, such as abandoned agricultural fields or degraded pastures. Food forestry harnesses the principles of secondary succession by mimicking natural processes to create a diverse, resilient, and low-maintenance ecosystem designed for food production. Rather than forcing annual crops year after year, which disrupts soil and ecological balance, food forests work with nature's successional stages to build a stable, self-sustaining community of plants, animals, and microorganisms. By carefully selecting species that will occupy different successional roles and fulfill various ecological functions—such as nitrogen fixation, pest control, pollination, and soil building—food forest practitioners can speed up the succession process to establish a productive ecosystem more quickly than if left entirely to nature.

In practical terms, creating a food forest often begins with early successional plants that prepare the soil and set the stage for long-term stability. These may include nitrogen-fixing shrubs, fast-growing ground covers, and hardy perennials, which improve soil fertility and structure. This early stage mimics the colonizing role of grasses and herbaceous plants in natural secondary succession. As the ecosystem matures, it progresses to include more complex, productive species, such as fruit and nut trees, perennial vegetables, and understory plants. Over time, this multi-layered structure emulates a natural forest ecosystem, with each plant occupying a specific layer and ecological niche, from towering canopy trees to ground-hugging herbs and root crops.

The benefits of a food forest modeled on secondary succession are significant. Because the system is diverse, it can more easily resist pests and diseases, as each plant and insect in the ecosystem plays a role in maintaining balance. The deep-rooted perennial plants and trees in later successional stages also help stabilize soil, reduce erosion, and improve water retention, creating a resilient system that requires minimal inputs once established. Moreover, the layered structure of a food forest maximizes sunlight capture and nutrients cycling, producing high yields in a relatively small space.

THE STAGES OF SUCCESSION IN A FOOD FOREST

A food forest evolves through several recognizable stages, each building on the last. The main stages include:

Pioneer Stage (Years 1-3)

The pioneer stage, spanning roughly years 1 to 3 in a food forest's development, initiates the process of ecological succession by establishing hardy, fast-growing species—known as pioneers—that can quickly colonize disturbed or barren soil. In nature, this stage marks the arrival of resilient plants capable of withstanding direct sunlight, poor soil conditions, and rapid environmental changes. In a food forest, the pioneer stage is equally critical, as it lays the groundwork for a thriving, sustainable ecosystem by enhancing soil health, drawing in pollinators, and facilitating nutrient cycling.

Pioneer species in a food forest are typically sun-loving, shallow-rooted plants that thrive in open, disturbed areas. They adapt readily to degraded or nutrient-poor soil, making them ideal for reestablishing a healthy environment after the ground has been cleared, tilled, or otherwise disrupted. These plants are usually annuals, biennials, or fast-growing perennials that grow quickly, set seed prolifically, and can tolerate the intense sunlight that characterizes open ground in the early stages of succession. Their rapid growth and abundant reproduction are essential in this stage, as they populate the soil, reduce erosion, and prevent invasive species from taking over by occupying available space. Common examples of annual pioneer plants include buckwheat, radishes, and sunflowers. These plants grow fast and die back quickly, contributing their organic matter to the soil, which enhances its structure and fertility. Perennials like clover, alfalfa, and lupines play a similar role but persist for several years, providing more sustained benefits. These species are particularly valuable as many are nitrogen-fixers, meaning they work with soil bacteria to convert atmospheric nitrogen into a form plants can use, thereby enriching the soil for future crops.

In addition to nitrogen fixation, many pioneer plants function as dynamic accumulators. These are plants with deep root systems that pull nutrients from the subsoil to the surface, depositing them in their leaves and stems. When these plants die or are pruned, they return these nutrients to the topsoil in an accessible form for other plants, thus jump-starting nutrient cycling within the ecosystem. This process is fundamental in a food forest, where building a rich, self-sustaining soil ecosystem is essential. By improving soil texture and adding organic matter, these pioneers transform the site from a barren or nutrient-poor landscape into a fertile environment capable of supporting a diverse range of species.

Beyond soil enhancement, pioneer species attract a variety of beneficial insects that play crucial roles in a food forest ecosystem. Their bright flowers, abundant nectar, and rapid turnover attract pollinators like bees and butterflies, as well as predatory insects that help manage pests. By bringing in these insects early in the forest's establishment, the pioneer stage encourages a balanced insect population that can keep pest species in check as the forest matures. Sunflowers, for example, are especially attractive to pollinators and predatory insects, creating a foundation of insect biodiversity that will benefit the entire forest ecosystem over time.

Shade is another important function of pioneer plants. As they grow, these species create a protective canopy over the soil, reducing temperature extremes and conserving moisture. This shading effect prepares the ground for the next successional wave of plants, often consisting of slower-growing shrubs, small trees, and longer-lived perennials that cannot tolerate the intense sunlight characteristic of open ground. By covering the soil, pioneers not only prevent erosion but also limit the emergence of weeds, making it easier for desired plant species to establish in later stages.

The pioneer stage is thus an essential foundation for the food forest, setting up a fertile, stable, and diverse environment. This stage doesn't just create soil that's rich in nutrients; it sets up an entire web of relationships among plants, insects, and soil organisms that will sustain the forest long after the initial pioneer species have been succeeded by more complex plant communities. As these pioneer plants mature, they continue to add organic matter to the soil through natural processes like leaf drop and decomposition, enriching the soil further and ensuring that subsequent plants have a well-prepared base.

Over time, as these pioneers complete their life cycle, they make way for longer-lived plants that require the richer soil and milder conditions created by the pioneers. Shrubs, fruiting perennials, and eventually, larger trees will begin to take over, forming the next stages of succession and leading to a mature, multilayered ecosystem that is resilient, productive, and self-sustaining. By carefully selecting and encouraging pioneer plants that serve multiple roles—soil building, nutrient cycling, pest control, and pollinator support—a food forest gardener can replicate nature's own strategies for ecosystem restoration and create a productive, sustainable system with minimal external inputs.

The pioneer stage, therefore, is not just a transient period but a vital phase of transformation that enables the entire food forest ecosystem to flourish. Through the integration of species that are both resilient and functional, the pioneer stage provides the foundation for a layered, complex, and mutually supportive community of plants, animals, and microorganisms. This approach leverages the power of ecological succession to develop a resilient food forest that can provide for humans while restoring and sustaining the land.

Building Phase (Years 4-6)

During the building phase, which spans years 4 to 6 in a food forest's development, the ecosystem begins to shift as pioneer species fulfill their role and gradually make way for more diverse and slightly longer-lived plants. This stage marks an essential transition from the fast-growing, sun-loving plants of the pioneer phase to an increasingly layered and complex community of perennials, shrubs, and early-succession trees that require slightly richer soil and can tolerate some shade. This phase sets the foundation for a more resilient and self-sustaining ecosystem by enhancing biodiversity, improving soil health, and introducing structural layers that support more specialized species.

The groundwork laid by pioneer species plays a crucial role in supporting this transition. As many of the fast-growing annuals and biennials begin to die back or complete their life cycle, they leave behind a wealth of organic matter, which enriches the soil. The decomposition of pioneer plants, along with the addition of leaf litter from early perennials, contributes to a buildup of organic material in the soil. This organic matter, along with the residues from nitrogen-fixing pioneers like clover and lupine, gradually creates humus—a stable form of organic matter that retains moisture and stores nutrients. As a result, the soil's water-holding capacity improves, nutrient cycling accelerates, and the soil structure becomes more hospitable to a range of life forms.

The increase in soil fertility attracts a variety of soil organisms, such as earthworms, fungi, and beneficial microorganisms, which further enhance soil health. Earthworms aerate the soil, breaking down organic material and leaving nutrient-rich castings that improve soil structure. Fungi, particularly mycorrhizal fungi, form symbiotic relationships with plant roots, helping them absorb nutrients more efficiently. This interaction between plants and fungi supports nutrient exchange within the ecosystem and strengthens plant resilience, as fungi can help plants withstand environmental stresses. These soil organisms are essential for establishing a robust soil food web, and their presence is a sign that the food forest ecosystem is maturing and becoming more resilient.

In the building phase, the introduction of early-succession perennials and shrubs marks the beginning of structural diversity in the food forest. These plants are still relatively sun-loving, but they are more demanding than pioneers in terms of soil quality, and they help fill in the forest's vertical structure by adding height and complexity. Early-succession perennials such as comfrey, artichoke, and asparagus thrive in the improved soil conditions. Comfrey, in particular, is a valuable addition due to its deep taproots, which draw up nutrients from the subsoil. As a dynamic accumulator, comfrey captures nutrients and makes them accessible to other plants when its leaves decompose. Perennial vegetables like artichoke and asparagus offer both edible yields and structural benefits, as their robust growth provides ground cover that helps retain moisture and suppress weeds.

Shrubs such as blackberries, raspberries, and elderberries are also introduced during this phase. These berry-producing plants not only provide food for humans but also attract pollinators and birds, adding biodiversity and further embedding the food forest into the surrounding environment. Their dense foliage and slightly woody structure contribute to the vertical layers that mimic a natural forest ecosystem. These shrubs play a dual role by providing habitat for small wildlife and beneficial insects while also supplying organic material through leaf litter, which decomposes and returns nutrients to the soil.

The introduction of nitrogen-fixing shrubs and small trees during the building phase further enriches the ecosystem. Species like the Siberian pea shrub and black locust contribute to soil fertility by forming symbiotic relationships with nitrogen-fixing bacteria, which convert atmospheric nitrogen into a form that plants can use. As these nitrogen-fixers grow and drop leaves or are pruned, they add nitrogen to the soil, enhancing the fertility for surrounding plants. Black locust, with its rapid growth and adaptability, is especially useful in this role, as it provides shade and wind protection for more delicate plants. Its flowers attract pollinators, while its nitrogen-fixing capabilities improve the surrounding soil, fostering an environment that benefits the entire plant community.

By the end of the building phase, the food forest has evolved into a more intricate ecosystem, with multiple layers of vegetation that contribute to a stable and productive environment. The interplay between soil health, structural complexity, and increased biodiversity has laid a solid foundation that supports a diverse community of plants, insects, and microorganisms. The presence of perennials, shrubs, and nitrogen-fixing trees fosters a continuous cycle of nutrient accumulation and release, which sustains plant growth without the need for chemical fertilizers. The diverse plantings attract a range of pollinators and beneficial insects, establishing a natural pest-control system that reduces the need for human intervention.

The building phase is essential not only for the growth of individual plants but also for the interconnected relationships that support the food forest's sustainability. Each new species introduced contributes to a web of interactions that strengthens the ecosystem's resilience. As the food forest matures beyond the building phase, it will continue to develop into a self-sustaining system that requires minimal input while offering maximum ecological and human benefits. This stage exemplifies the power of ecological succession in creating a layered, diverse, and balanced ecosystem that can thrive in harmony with its natural surroundings.

Shrub Layer Expansion (Years 6-10)

During the shrub layer expansion phase, spanning years 6 to 10 in the development of a food forest, the ecosystem matures significantly, supporting a denser and more diverse range of shrubs and small trees. This phase marks a shift from a landscape dominated by low-lying vegetation and pioneer species to one where mid-sized shrubs, small trees, and the earliest canopy species come into their own. As soil fertility, organic matter, and soil structure have improved from the groundwork laid in previous phases, the ecosystem can now sustain more complex species, enhancing biodiversity and establishing a resilient, self-sustaining environment.

One of the most notable introductions during this phase is fruit-bearing shrubs and small trees, which bring both ecological and human benefits. By introducing varieties like hazelnuts, blueberries, currants, and serviceberries, the food forest begins to produce a range of edible yields while also supporting wildlife. These shrubs add complexity to the food forest, creating layers that mimic the structure of natural woodlands. Hazelnuts, for example, offer a nutritious food source and establish robust root systems that help prevent soil erosion, while blueberries and currants provide berries that attract pollinators and birds. Serviceberries contribute to early spring blooms, supporting bees and other pollinators, and their berries add another source of food later in the season. These fruit-bearing shrubs contribute to an increasing diversity in plant species, which supports a balanced ecosystem less susceptible to disease and pests.

As shrub density grows, so does the habitat quality for wildlife. This phase of development attracts a variety of birds, insects, and small mammals, which in turn contribute to the health and resilience of the food forest. Birds are valuable allies in natural pest control, feeding on insects that might otherwise harm the plants. Birds also contribute to seed dispersion, helping new plants take root across the forest. Small mammals, too, play a role, aiding in the dispersal of seeds and organic matter as they move about, inadvertently enriching the soil with their waste and the organic material they displace. The increase in shrub density also benefits beneficial insects such as bees, hoverflies, and predatory beetles, which find shelter within the foliage and contribute to pollination and pest control.

The expanding shrub layer in this stage also begins to modify the microclimate within the food forest. With more foliage, the forest becomes adept at moderating temperatures, holding moisture, and providing shelter from wind and harsh weather conditions. As these mid-story plants create shade, they reduce direct sunlight on the soil, helping to retain soil moisture and creating conditions suitable for more shade-tolerant and moisture-loving species. The canopy now becomes layered, with the overlapping foliage of shrubs and young trees offering different levels of sunlight exposure, which encourages diverse plant growth from the ground layer up through the mid-story. This layering effect, in addition to providing various habitats for wildlife, creates a buffer against the extremes of sun, wind, and rain, ensuring that the younger, more sensitive plants below have a better chance to thrive. The layered canopy structure also limits the impact of heavy rainfall on the soil, helping to prevent erosion while retaining nutrients within the ecosystem.

The increased complexity of the shrub and tree layer allows the food forest to rely even less on human intervention, as natural processes within the ecosystem begin to maintain balance. The plant diversity creates a natural defense against pests and diseases; where monoculture can lead to vulnerability, the varied species and plant structures here ensure that any pest or disease affecting one species is less likely to spread. Nitrogen-fixing shrubs and trees, such as certain varieties of alder or Siberian pea shrub introduced earlier, continue to replenish the soil, supporting nutrient cycling and reducing the need for external fertilizers. The growing interdependence of plants and animals builds a self-sustaining system in which nutrient, water, and pest control cycles operate with minimal human input.

By the end of the shrub layer expansion phase, the food forest has developed a multi-layered, diverse, and resilient structure that mimics a natural forest. The higher density of shrubs, the introduction of small fruiting trees, and the enriched habitats foster a vibrant ecosystem that promotes biodiversity, supports wildlife, and provides a sustainable yield of food and resources. This ecosystem complexity not only strengthens the food forest's resilience but also allows it to become increasingly productive and self-maintaining. The food forest is now able to support not only human needs for food but also provides essential ecosystem services, from carbon sequestration and soil building to wildlife habitat and water retention.

The establishment of these shrub and small tree layers ensures that the food forest is set up for long-term growth. As these plants mature and start to reach their full height and productive potential, they pave the way for even larger canopy trees that may be introduced in subsequent years, completing the forest's vertical structure. The success of the shrub layer expansion stage marks the food forest's evolution from a young, developing ecosystem into a mature, stable, and productive landscape. Each plant, animal, and microorganism now plays an integrated role in a system that, with time, will continue to adapt, evolve, and sustain itself as a thriving forest ecosystem.

Developing Tree Canopy (Years 10-20)

As the food forest continues to mature between the 10 to 20-year mark, the system undergoes significant changes, especially as larger trees begin to establish themselves and form a partial canopy. This stage represents a transition toward a fully integrated and multi-layered forest structure, which mirrors natural ecosystems found in mature forests. With the creation of this canopy, the forest starts to stabilize, developing a complex and resilient ecosystem that thrives with minimal intervention. Shade-tolerant plants that struggled under the full sun of earlier phases now begin to flourish beneath the emerging tree canopy, further diversifying the landscape. This process is accompanied by an intensification of nutrient cycling, and the health of the soil reaches its peak, ensuring that the food forest can sustain its own growth over the long term.

The establishment of canopy trees, including fruit and nut trees like apple, pear, peach, chestnut, and walnut, marks the beginning of a significant shift in the forest's structure. These trees not only add vertical layers to the forest but also contribute to its longevity and productivity. As the trees grow larger, they start to bear fruit, providing substantial yields while also enriching the food forest in other ways. These trees, with their deep root systems, play a crucial role in stabilizing the soil, preventing erosion, and improving water retention. Their ability to produce food is vital for both human and wildlife needs, as they provide diverse and seasonal crops that attract pollinators, birds, and mammals. The addition of fruit and nut trees introduces a higher level of biodiversity and complexity to the food forest, creating niches for a variety of organisms and strengthening the overall resilience of the system.

Alongside the growth of canopy trees, the understory layer develops, adding even more layers to the food forest structure. Shade-tolerant species like currants, gooseberries, and edible groundcovers such as wild ginger, violets, and strawberries begin to thrive beneath the partial canopy. These plants, which were previously unable to survive in the direct sunlight of earlier stages, now benefit from the protection of the taller trees. The reduced sunlight allows these understory plants to thrive, providing a diverse range of edible crops that complement the fruiting trees above. The presence of these plants enhances the biodiversity of the food forest, as they attract different types of pollinators and beneficial insects, which in turn contribute to pest control. These groundcovers also help to retain moisture in the soil, preventing it from drying out during the warmer months and ensuring that the ecosystem remains stable.

In addition to the growth of canopy trees and understory plants, the depth and diversity of the root systems increase, contributing to more efficient nutrient cycling and soil health. As the canopy trees grow, their deep roots draw nutrients from the deeper layers of the soil and bring them to the surface, where they are made available to other plants. This rooting depth helps balance the soil by improving its structure and fertility, ensuring that nutrients are distributed evenly throughout the system. The diverse root systems also play a key role in stabilizing the soil, preventing erosion, and supporting the microbial life that is crucial for maintaining soil health. The increased organic matter in the soil, generated by the decaying roots and fallen leaves, supports a thriving ecosystem of fungi, bacteria, and worms that further enhance nutrient cycling. These processes create a self-sustaining system in which plants, animals, and microorganisms all play interconnected roles in maintaining the health and productivity of the ecosystem.

The nutrient cycling in the food forest reaches its peak during this phase, as the layers of organic material from the trees, shrubs, and groundcovers break down and return essential nutrients to the soil. This cycle of growth, decay, and renewal is what sustains the food forest, ensuring that it can continue to support a wide variety of plant and animal life over time. The increased organic matter and microbial activity in the soil result in improved soil structure, which enhances water retention and allows plants to access the nutrients they need. As the food forest matures, the ecosystem becomes more efficient at self-regulation, with little need for external inputs like fertilizers or pesticides. The system becomes a model of sustainability, where the diversity of plant species, the complexity of the forest structure, and the interdependent relationships between plants, animals, and microorganisms ensure that the forest can thrive on its own.

As the tree canopy continues to grow and expand, the food forest evolves into a more productive and resilient ecosystem. The combination of fruit and nut trees, understory plants, and diverse root systems creates a forest that can provide food, habitat, and ecological services, all while maintaining its health and vitality. The development of the canopy during this phase is not just a visual transformation; it is the foundation for the next stages of the food forest's life, where larger trees and further complexity will eventually lead to a fully developed forest ecosystem. This multi-layered structure, with its diverse plant and animal life, will continue to grow and adapt, providing sustainable yields for generations to come while enriching the surrounding environment.

Climax or Mature Forest Stage (20+ years)

The climax or mature forest stage marks the final and most stable phase in the development of a food forest, typically occurring after 20 years or more. At this point, the system has evolved into a fully integrated ecosystem with complex layers of vegetation, ranging from tall canopy trees to groundcovers, creating a well-balanced environment that requires little to no human intervention. This stage is defined by maximum ecological stability and resilience, where the food forest reaches its highest potential in terms of productivity, biodiversity, and sustainability.

One of the key features of the climax stage is the establishment of multiple layers of vegetation. The canopy layer is now fully developed, with large trees providing shade and shelter for the layers beneath. These trees, often fruit and nut varieties such as apples, pears, walnuts, and chestnuts, contribute to the diversity and stability of the forest by providing food and habitat for a variety of species. Beneath the canopy, the understory trees and shrubs thrive, their smaller size and shade tolerance allowing them to grow in the filtered light. These include plants like currants, gooseberries, and smaller fruit trees, which continue to provide food sources for both humans and wildlife. The herbaceous layer, consisting of perennial herbs and groundcovers, also flourishes, providing additional diversity in terms of both plant species and the ecological functions they perform. Vines and root crops fill out the lower layers, creating a rich and intricate web of vegetation that supports a wide variety of organisms.

The diverse plant layers in the mature food forest create an array of microhabitats, each with its own unique conditions and ecological functions. Microclimates—areas with slightly different temperature, humidity, and light conditions—are now a common feature, as the layered vegetation creates pockets of shade, moisture, and warmth in different parts of the forest. These microhabitats support a variety of animal and insect populations, including pollinators, predators, and beneficial insects. The presence of different plant species at various heights and growing conditions offers food, shelter, and breeding grounds for a wide range of organisms. Birds, mammals, amphibians, and insects all thrive in this rich environment, each playing a role in maintaining the ecological balance. For example, pollinators like bees and butterflies are supported by the flowering plants, while beneficial insects such as ladybugs and parasitic wasps help control pests that might otherwise threaten the health of the plants.

In addition to the diverse microhabitats, the mature food forest also benefits from a complex and highly efficient soil food web. This web includes microorganisms such as bacteria, fungi, and worms, all of which play a crucial role in breaking down organic matter and cycling nutrients back into the soil. At the climax stage, the forest operates as a self-sustaining system, with minimal external inputs required. The decomposition of plant material—such as fallen leaves, dead branches, and decaying roots—creates a constant supply of organic matter that enriches the soil. This organic material is broken down by fungi and bacteria, which release nutrients into the soil, making them available to the plants. The roots of the plants, in turn, exude substances that support microbial life and help maintain soil structure. This closed-loop nutrient cycle ensures that the food forest remains fertile and productive without the need for synthetic fertilizers or other artificial inputs.

As the food forest reaches its climax, the system also becomes increasingly resilient to disturbances, whether natural or human-induced. The complex layers of vegetation, the diversity of species, and the established nutrient cycles all contribute to the stability of the system. If a tree falls or a plant dies, the system can absorb the impact and continue functioning without significant disruption. The food forest is now a dynamic, self-regulating ecosystem that can withstand fluctuations in weather, pests, and diseases. This resilience is further enhanced by the variety of species present; with so many different plants and animals occupying different niches, the system is less vulnerable to the collapse of any one part. For example, if one species of plant is affected by a pest or disease, others can fill the gap, ensuring that the overall productivity and health of the forest are maintained.

The climax stage of a food forest represents the culmination of years of growth, succession, and ecological development. It is a phase of abundance and harmony, where the plants, animals, and microorganisms interact in a balanced and mutually beneficial way. The forest becomes a thriving, self-sustaining system that provides food, shelter, and ecological services with minimal human intervention. At this stage, the food forest is not only a productive and diverse ecosystem but also a model of sustainability, demonstrating how human cultivation can coexist with nature in a way that supports both ecological health and human well-being. With its multiple layers of vegetation, rich biodiversity, and self-sustaining nutrient cycles, the mature food forest is a testament to the power of nature's processes and the potential of agroforestry systems.

DESIGNING A FOOD FOREST WITH SUCCESSION IN MIND

Designing a food forest with succession in mind requires careful planning to ensure that the ecosystem develops in a way that mimics natural processes while providing diverse yields and ecological benefits. The concept of succession is central to the process, as it represents the natural progression of plant and soil development over time. By aligning your food forest design with these stages of ecological succession, you can create a self-sustaining system that improves soil health, increases biodiversity, and produces food for years to come.

The process begins with laying a solid foundation by introducing pioneer species and nitrogen-fixing plants during the early years. These plants are essential for improving soil quality, creating habitats, and providing organic matter. Pioneer species, typically fast-growing annuals or early perennials, thrive in disturbed soils and have the ability to break down organic matter, which gradually enriches the soil. Nitrogen-fixing plants, such as clover, alfalfa, or legumes, play a crucial role in replenishing the soil with nitrogen, an essential nutrient that plants need for growth. By introducing these species early in the design, you not only begin the process of soil enrichment but also start to establish a habitat that attracts pollinators and beneficial insects, laying the groundwork for future plantings.

As the system begins to stabilize and the soil improves, you can gradually introduce perennials and shrubs into the food forest. These plants are more long-lived than the pioneers and help increase the structural complexity of the ecosystem. Shrubs, berry-producing plants, and early-fruiting species are important for both food production and ecological functions. These species serve multiple roles—they provide food for both humans and wildlife, attract pollinators, and offer shelter for beneficial insects, birds, and small mammals. These plants also continue the process of soil improvement by adding organic matter and providing deeper root systems that stabilize the soil. By gradually introducing these species, you can ensure that your food forest has a balance of early- and mid-successional plants that work together to build a more diverse and stable system.

As the food forest matures, the plant layers should diversify, with the addition of more shade-tolerant species that can thrive beneath the canopy. These plants, such as medicinal herbs, berry bushes, and groundcovers, are suited to the increasing shade provided by maturing trees and shrubs. The gradual introduction of shade-tolerant plants is important for creating a multi-layered system that mimics the complexity of natural forests. Over time, the ground layer, including herbs and groundcovers, becomes more established, creating a thick, rich layer of vegetation that helps with moisture retention, reduces weeds, and adds organic matter to the soil. These plants, while contributing to food production, also support the overall ecosystem by improving soil health, promoting biodiversity, and fostering beneficial insect populations.

A critical component of your food forest design is planning for the growth of the tree canopy. Canopy trees, which provide shade and shelter for the layers beneath, need careful consideration in terms of their size, light requirements, and spacing. When designing your food forest, consider the ultimate size of the trees and their light requirements, as well as how they will affect the amount of sunlight that reaches lower layers as they mature.

Space the trees thoughtfully to allow sunlight to filter through the upper canopy and reach the understory and herbaceous layers for as long as possible. This allows you to maximize food production in the lower layers while ensuring that the canopy trees have enough space to grow without overcrowding one another. The careful selection of tree species that provide food, shade, and ecological benefits will enhance the biodiversity of the food forest, ensuring that the system remains productive for years to come.

Finally, as your food forest matures and becomes more self-sufficient, human intervention should decrease. The goal is to create a system that mimics the low-maintenance nature of natural ecosystems, where minimal weeding, fertilization, or pest control is required. By focusing on building a healthy, resilient ecosystem that supports a wide range of species, your food forest should be able to maintain its own balance without the need for constant human input. This is achieved through the establishment of diverse plant layers, robust nutrient cycles, and natural pest control mechanisms. As the system becomes more established, it will naturally regulate itself, with beneficial insects controlling pests and the soil food web ensuring the availability of nutrients for plant growth.

Incorporating the principles of succession into your food forest design ensures that the system develops in a way that is both ecologically sound and productive. By starting with a solid foundation of pioneer species, gradually introducing perennials and shrubs, diversifying plant layers over time, and planning for canopy growth, you can create a resilient, self-sustaining ecosystem. As the food forest matures, it will become increasingly independent, requiring minimal intervention while continuing to provide food, habitat, and ecological benefits for years to come.

ECOLOGICAL BENEFITS OF NATURAL SUCCESSION IN A FOOD FOREST

The ecological benefits of natural succession in a food forest are vast, as each stage of succession creates a dynamic and interdependent system that nurtures biodiversity, improves soil health, and enhances overall ecosystem resilience. By mimicking the natural processes of succession, a food forest becomes a self-sustaining environment that is less reliant on external inputs, offering a range of ecological advantages.

One of the most significant benefits of ecological succession in a food forest is the increased biodiversity it supports. As the forest matures, different plant species establish themselves at various stages of succession, creating a layered and complex ecosystem. This variety of plant life attracts a wide range of insects, birds, and animals, forming a food web that enhances the overall resilience of the system. Each layer in the food forest, from the groundcovers to the canopy, hosts unique species, creating microhabitats and ecological niches. This diversity not only provides habitats and food sources for wildlife but also strengthens the system's ability to resist pests, diseases, and environmental stresses. A rich diversity of species makes it more likely that some will thrive even when others face challenges, ensuring the ecosystem remains stable and productive.

Another key benefit is the improvement of soil health. As different plant species establish themselves over time, organic matter builds up in the soil, which is crucial for maintaining fertility and structure. Pioneer species like legumes and other nitrogen-fixing plants play a particularly important role in enriching the soil by adding nitrogen, an essential nutrient for plant growth. As plants mature, their roots penetrate deeper into the soil, helping to break up compacted layers and improve water infiltration. Additionally, the decaying plant material, roots, and animal waste contribute to the accumulation of organic matter, enhancing the soil's ability to retain nutrients and moisture. This process leads to a rich, well-structured soil that supports healthy plant growth and promotes a sustainable ecosystem.

Efficient nutrient cycling is another ecological benefit that arises from natural succession in a food forest. In a well-balanced ecosystem, the nutrients required for plant growth are continually recycled. As plants and animals die, their decomposition releases nutrients back into the soil, where they are taken up by living plants. This cycle is enhanced by the presence of a variety of plants with different root depths and nutrient requirements. The diversity of plant species ensures that nutrients are efficiently utilized and redistributed throughout the system. Over time, the food forest becomes increasingly self-sustaining, with fewer external inputs needed to maintain soil fertility.

Natural pest control is a vital ecological service provided by a food forest in succession. By fostering a habitat that supports a wide range of beneficial insects, such as ladybugs, predatory wasps, and spiders, a food forest creates a natural balance between pests and their predators. These insects help keep pest populations in check, reducing the need for chemical pesticides or manual pest control. Furthermore, the complex structure of the food forest, with its dense layers of vegetation, offers shelter and resources for these beneficial organisms. By maintaining a healthy population of predators and parasitoids, the food forest naturally controls pest outbreaks, contributing to the overall health of the system.

Finally, the resilience of a food forest to climate extremes is enhanced through its layered structure. A mature food forest provides microclimates that protect plants from extreme temperatures, wind, and rainfall. The canopy trees offer shade and shelter to the understory, while the dense groundcover reduces the impact of soil erosion and helps retain moisture. These layers of protection allow the food forest to withstand periods of drought, heavy rainfall, or extreme heat, ensuring the long-term stability and productivity of the system. As the ecosystem matures, its ability to adapt to changing environmental conditions strengthens, making it more resilient to the impacts of climate change.

In summary, the ecological benefits of natural succession in a food forest are numerous and interrelated. The increase in biodiversity, improvement in soil health, efficient nutrient cycling, natural pest control, and resilience to climate extremes all contribute to the creation of a self-sustaining, low-maintenance ecosystem. As the food forest matures, it becomes an increasingly stable and productive environment, capable of supporting a diverse range of species while providing food and ecological services for generations to come.

MANAGING SUCCESSION IN A FOOD FOREST

Managing succession in a food forest is vital for creating a resilient and self-sustaining ecosystem that not only produces food but also enriches the surrounding landscape. Ecological succession, which involves the gradual replacement of species and the buildup of soil, often takes decades to reach its natural maturity. However, in a food forest, the aim is to harness and accelerate this process to establish a diverse, productive system that mirrors natural forests. Effective management of succession requires careful selection, timing, and integration of plants and practices at each phase to maximize benefits and maintain ecological balance.

The first step in managing succession is to set clear goals for each stage of the food forest's development. In the early pioneer stage, the primary goal is to establish ground cover, build initial soil health, control weeds, and begin nutrient cycling. This is accomplished by introducing hardy, fast-growing species like legumes and dynamic accumulators, which fix nitrogen and improve soil fertility. As the system transitions into the building phase, the focus shifts to increasing plant diversity, improving soil fertility further, and introducing long-lived perennials and shrubs. These plants add complexity to the ecosystem while supporting both food production and ecological roles like attracting pollinators. The next stage, the shrub layer expansion, focuses on integrating edible shrubs, deepening root systems, and creating habitats for beneficial organisms. As larger fruit and nut trees are introduced in the developing tree canopy stage, the goal is to expand shade tolerance, increase stability, and prepare the system for the final, mature forest stage. At maturity, the food forest should be self-sustaining, with minimal human intervention required to maintain its health and productivity.

Designing a food forest with succession in mind is key to ensuring a smooth transition between each phase. This begins with planting in layers, from the canopy down to the groundcover, creating a multi-layered forest system that uses light and resources efficiently. Planning for the light and shade requirements of each plant is also essential. Initially, sun-loving plants are planted, with more shade-tolerant species introduced as the canopy develops. Proper spacing is critical to ensure plants have enough room to grow, especially trees and shrubs that need more space for their root systems. Companion planting helps maximize space and can reduce competition, as well as suppress allelopathic effects that certain plants may have on others.

In the pioneer stage, soil-building and fertility are top priorities. Plants like clover, alfalfa, and comfrey not only fix nitrogen but also attract beneficial insects and suppress weeds. These plants lay the groundwork for the next stages of succession by improving soil health and creating a solid foundation for future growth. As the building phase progresses, the food forest starts to diversify. Shrubs like raspberries, elderberries, and currants are introduced, as well as nitrogen-fixing species that continue to enhance the soil. The goal here is to create a balanced system with a variety of plant species at different growth stages. During this time, it's important to remove or prune pioneer plants that begin to overcrowd or outcompete newer, more permanent species.

As the shrub layer expands, a focus on edible shrubs and small fruiting plants enhances food production and biodiversity. This stage also introduces plants that thrive in partial shade, preparing the forest for the canopy trees that will eventually dominate the space. Shrubs play a critical role in creating habitat for wildlife, while also adding structure to the ecosystem. By this stage, the canopy trees are introduced, but it's important to manage sunlight levels carefully to ensure that the lower layers of the forest continue to thrive. The final stages of development see the establishment of mature trees that provide long-term food sources and shade. The food forest begins to form a fully developed, layered ecosystem, with each level supporting the others.

The climax stage, or the mature forest, is where the food forest achieves a state of ecological balance. Here, the system is largely self-sustaining, with minimal human intervention needed to maintain the ecosystem. Nutrient cycling becomes efficient as fallen leaves and plant material decompose, returning nutrients to the soil. At this point, regular pruning and thinning may still be necessary to maintain light levels and prevent overcrowding, but the food forest will have reached a stage where it requires very little ongoing maintenance. Regular observation and adaptive management are crucial throughout the entire process. Monitoring how plants are growing, how well they are competing, and the effectiveness of the system in supporting biodiversity allows for adjustments when needed. Over time, you may need to thin plants, adjust for changes in soil conditions, or foster biodiversity if certain species are underrepresented.

Ultimately, managing succession in a food forest requires thoughtful planning, ongoing observation, and a hands-off approach once the system is mature. By guiding your food forest through each phase of succession and creating a multi-layered, diverse ecosystem, you can cultivate a resilient, self-sustaining environment that supports food production and promotes ecological health for years to come.

CHAPTER EIGHT

FOREST GARDENING SYSTEMS

Food forest gardening (or forest gardening) is a perennial, polycultural system that mimics natural ecosystems, integrating a diverse range of edible plants, medicinal herbs, and beneficial species within layers similar to those found in natural forests. This holistic approach to gardening maximizes productivity, self-sufficiency, and sustainability by using natural principles of succession, plant diversity, and soil health. Here's an in-depth exploration of the food forest gardening system, its principles, layers, and best practices for its establishment and maintenance.

Principles of Food Forest Gardening Systems

Food forest gardening is a sustainable approach to agriculture that focuses on creating self-sustaining ecosystems similar to natural forests. By mimicking the structure and functions of forests, food forests provide a resilient, low-maintenance food production system that requires minimal human intervention after establishment. This approach to food production aims not only to yield crops but also to support ecological health, soil fertility, biodiversity, and natural pest management. The principles of food forest gardening emphasize designing ecosystems that sustain themselves while delivering diverse food resources.

At the core of food forest gardening is the idea of mimicking natural ecosystems. Food forests are modeled on the resilience and efficiency of forest systems, which operate without significant external inputs. By replicating the structure of natural forests, food forests are able to sustain themselves with minimal human assistance, relying on diverse plant species that work together to improve soil fertility, conserve water, and naturally deter pests. This diversity of species and ecosystem functions means that food forests can thrive in ways that are similar to wild forests, offering a reliable source of food while benefiting the surrounding environment. In a food forest, plants are selected based on their ecological functions as much as their yield, creating a balanced and resilient system.

Another fundamental principle of food forests is their emphasis on perennial and polycultural plant systems. Unlike traditional annual crop systems that require replanting each season, food forests prioritize perennials, plants that regrow year after year. This approach reduces the labor and energy involved in replanting and tilling the soil each season, allowing the system to establish deeper roots and build more complex soil ecosystems over time. In addition to perennials, food forests use polycultures—combinations of multiple plant species grown together in the same area. This diversity of plants promotes a more stable ecosystem by encouraging various forms of life to coexist and interact. Polycultural designs enhance biodiversity, which strengthens the resilience of the ecosystem to pests, diseases, and weather changes. The result is a productive system that, over time, requires less input and management from humans.

A defining characteristic of food forests is their layered structure, known as stratification. Like natural forests, food forests are composed of multiple layers, each fulfilling a unique ecological role and making use of different spaces within the ecosystem. These layers typically include canopy trees that provide shade and fruit; understory trees that benefit from partial shade; shrubs that produce berries; herbaceous plants for ground cover and smaller yields; ground covers to protect the soil surface; vines that use vertical space; and root crops that occupy the underground layer. This stratified approach allows the food forest to maximize vertical space, capture sunlight more efficiently, and support a high level of biodiversity within a limited area. By utilizing each layer to its fullest, food forests create a diverse ecosystem that mimics the complex layering found in natural forests, enabling them to host a wide range of plants, insects, and microorganisms that each contribute to the overall health and productivity of the system.

The concept of symbiosis and mutual support is also key in food forest gardening. In these systems, plants are chosen for their ability to support one another through natural relationships, such as nitrogen-fixing plants that improve soil for nearby species or plants that attract beneficial insects that control pests. These complementary relationships between species enhance growth and resilience across the ecosystem. By encouraging mutual support among plants, food forests reduce the need for chemical inputs like fertilizers and pesticides, as plants help each other thrive. Insects and animals also play essential roles in food forests, often forming beneficial relationships that further support the growth and productivity of the ecosystem. Birds, for example, can help control pest populations, while pollinators like bees facilitate the reproduction of flowering plants. This interconnected web of life forms a balanced and sustainable ecosystem where each species contributes to the health of the others, ultimately supporting the productivity of the food forest as a whole.

A self-sustaining, minimal input design is one of the most appealing aspects of food forests, especially in contrast to conventional agriculture, which often relies heavily on fertilizers, pesticides, and tilling. In a food forest, the initial setup and plant selection are carefully planned to allow natural processes to handle soil fertility, pest management, and weed suppression without continuous external inputs. Perennial plants reduce the need for annual tilling, which can disrupt soil structure and lead to erosion. Moreover, the presence of diverse plant species that fill various ecological roles naturally reduces the likelihood of pest outbreaks or nutrient deficiencies, making the system more self-sufficient. As a result, food forests generally require far less labor and resource input after they are established, offering a sustainable alternative that respects and works within natural processes.

The long-term focus of food forest gardening is another defining principle. These systems are designed to improve with age as plants mature and the ecosystem becomes increasingly stable and productive. In contrast to annual farming systems that need to be replanted and heavily managed each year, food forests are intended to yield benefits that grow over time. As perennial plants establish deeper roots, they improve soil health, retain more water, and enhance nutrient cycling within the ecosystem. This leads to a more stable and productive system that can produce consistent yields with less input as the years go by. The gradual buildup of organic matter from fallen leaves, decomposing plants, and other natural processes creates a rich soil layer that continuously supports plant growth, allowing the food forest to thrive independently.

In essence, food forest gardening is a holistic approach to sustainable agriculture that integrates ecological principles to create a self-sustaining, productive ecosystem. By mimicking natural forest systems, prioritizing perennials, using a stratified structure, fostering symbiotic relationships, minimizing external inputs, and focusing on long-term productivity, food forests offer a resilient, environmentally friendly method of food production. This approach not only yields crops but also supports biodiversity, soil health, and ecosystem stability, making it a valuable model for sustainable land management. Over time, a well-designed food forest can provide a steady supply of food while enhancing the surrounding environment, embodying the principles of regenerative agriculture and ecological harmony.

FOOD FOREST MODELS

Orchard Based

An orchard-based food forest model is a type of food forest that centers around fruit and nut trees as the primary canopy layer, blending the traditional concept of an orchard with the layered, diverse planting of a food forest. In this model, fruit and nut trees serve as the core of the system, with other plants organized in layers beneath and around them. This approach provides multiple ecological and agricultural benefits, creating a biodiverse, resilient, and productive system that requires minimal inputs once established.

Features of the Orchard-Based Food Forest Model

An orchard-based food forest model integrates the structured planting of traditional orchards with the layered, polycultural diversity of a food forest to create a biodiverse, resilient, and productive system. The primary focus of this model is on the canopy layer of fruit and nut trees, such as apples, pears, chestnuts, walnuts, and peaches. These trees form the foundation of the system, providing the primary food yield while creating a canopy that supports the growth of various plant layers beneath. While the tree-focused canopy structure organizes plantings in a pattern similar to an orchard, it includes additional layers to mimic natural forest ecosystems. This approach brings several benefits by enhancing biodiversity, increasing resilience, and improving productivity.

The layered design of an orchard-based food forest reflects natural ecosystems, where various plant species coexist in vertical and horizontal arrangements that utilize every available space. Rather than limiting production to rows of fruit or nut trees, this model incorporates a range of plants, including shrubs, herbs, ground covers, vines, and root crops that grow at different heights and spread across different zones. This layered design maximizes sunlight capture, water retention, and nutrient cycling, as plants with different structures and root depths interact with each other, improving the entire system's overall health and productivity. The presence of multiple layers, from the canopy down to the root zone, means the food forest can sustain a diversity of crops and functional plants within a single area, providing benefits to soil, plants, and ecosystem stability.

The orchard-based food forest is also rich in edible and functional diversity. The variety of plants within this system is not just limited to edible species; it includes medicinal and beneficial plants that improve ecosystem health. For instance, nitrogen-fixing plants like clover or autumn olive can improve soil fertility by naturally enriching it with nitrogen, reducing the need for external fertilizers. Pest-repellent plants, such as marigolds or garlic, can protect fruit and nut trees from harmful insects, while pollinator-attracting plants like bee balm or coneflower increase the presence of bees and other pollinators necessary for fruit production. This mix of plants around the orchard trees increases the range of products yielded by the food forest while simultaneously fostering a healthy, balanced ecosystem. This functional diversity provides an integrated approach to managing soil fertility, pests, and pollination without requiring synthetic chemicals or intensive inputs.

Natural pest management and soil fertility are additional critical aspects of the orchard-based food forest model. Companion plants and beneficial insects are essential to a self-sustaining pest control strategy. Companion plants act as a natural barrier against harmful pests, while flowers and herbs that attract predatory insects, such as ladybugs or parasitic wasps, help control pest populations. In this way, the food forest's biodiversity contributes directly to its resilience, reducing the need for chemical interventions and creating a healthier environment for the plants and wildlife within it. The model also incorporates perennial ground covers and mulch to maintain soil health. Ground covers such as clover or creeping thyme help suppress weeds and protect the soil from erosion, while organic mulches break down over time to add nutrients back into the soil, supporting the ecosystem's long-term fertility.

In addition to pest control, this design prioritizes soil fertility, achieved through a mix of mulch, nitrogen-fixing plants, and strategic plant choices that support nutrient recycling. As perennial ground covers protect the soil and conserve moisture, mulch from organic material like straw, wood chips, or decomposing plant matter serves as a continuous source of organic material for soil organisms. These soil organisms, such as earthworms and beneficial fungi, break down organic matter and recycle nutrients back into the soil, supporting plant growth. Nitrogen-fixing plants work in a similar way, contributing valuable nitrogen that other plants can absorb, thereby minimizing the need for synthetic fertilizers.

The orchard-based food forest model offers a comprehensive, ecosystem-based approach to sustainable agriculture. By combining an orchard's structured canopy with a food forest's diversity of supportive plant layers, this model optimizes productivity, conserves resources, and builds resilience. Its layered structure uses vertical and horizontal planting spaces to increase the productivity of each square foot, while functional diversity within the system strengthens natural defenses against pests and diseases. Natural pest management, soil enrichment, and water conservation are all enhanced by plant interactions, reducing the need for external inputs and lowering maintenance requirements over time. As a result, the orchard-based food forest not only provides a sustainable source of fruits, nuts, herbs, and vegetables but also supports long-term soil health, increases biodiversity, and creates a self-sustaining agricultural system that is resilient to environmental stresses.

This integration of structure and function makes the orchard-based food forest a powerful model for sustainable food production. By leveraging the benefits of natural ecosystems, this model establishes a productive landscape that requires less labor and chemical input as it matures. Through the symbiotic relationships of plants, insects, and soil organisms, it achieves a balance that supports both high-yield crops and ecological health. This approach not only meets human food needs but also contributes positively to the environment by building soil fertility, sequestering carbon, and creating habitats for wildlife. Over time, as trees and other perennial plants establish deep roots and soil health improves, the orchard-based food forest evolves into a stable, resilient system capable of providing an abundant, low-maintenance food source that mirrors the productivity and diversity of a natural forest.

Layers in the Orchard-Based Food Forest Model

The orchard-based food forest model brings together the structured layout of an orchard with the diversity and ecological design of a food forest. Central to this model is the layering of plants, a technique that mimics natural ecosystems by using seven distinct plant layers to create a self-sustaining and productive environment. Each layer is carefully selected and strategically arranged to support the canopy of fruit and nut trees while fostering a balanced ecosystem. The result is a productive landscape that maximizes sunlight, water retention, soil fertility, and biodiversity, creating a healthy system that produces a variety of yields throughout the growing season.

The canopy layer forms the heart of the orchard-based food forest, featuring mainstay fruit and nut trees such as apple, pear, plum, peach, chestnut, almond, walnut, and pecan. These trees are essential not only for their high yields of fruit and nuts but also for their structural role in the system, providing shade and creating a microclimate that benefits the layers beneath. By controlling temperature and humidity, the canopy trees establish an environment where diverse plant life can thrive. Typically, these trees are spaced with sufficient intervals to ensure ample air circulation and light penetration, essential factors for maintaining tree health and preventing disease. This uppermost layer is the backbone of the orchard food forest, defining its spatial structure and providing a range of food, shade, and habitat for wildlife.

Beneath the canopy, the understory layer consists of smaller fruit and nut trees like dwarf apple varieties, pawpaw, hazelnut, fig, and elderberry. These trees thrive in partial shade, creating a seamless transition from the canopy above to the layers below. The understory trees serve to increase the diversity and complexity of the orchard-based system, adding yields of nuts, fruits, and berries while occupying the spaces between larger trees. By creating a buffer between the canopy and lower layers, these understory trees contribute to a more resilient and productive ecosystem. Their presence encourages biodiversity, which improves the system's overall health and resilience to environmental changes.

Next is the shrub layer, populated with berry bushes and nitrogen-fixing shrubs such as blueberries, raspberries, blackberries, currants, autumn olive, and goumi. The shrub layer provides an accessible yield of berries and other small fruits while enriching the soil. Nitrogen-fixing shrubs are particularly valuable in this layer, as they draw nitrogen from the atmosphere and make it available in the soil, nourishing nearby plants and reducing the need for external fertilizers. The presence of berry bushes also attracts pollinators, birds, and beneficial insects, which contribute to natural pest control and enhance biodiversity. By supporting a diversity of plant life and animal species, the shrub layer strengthens the overall ecosystem health and productivity.

The herbaceous layer, comprised of culinary and medicinal herbs such as mint, basil, thyme, comfrey, sage, and bee balm, adds both utility and ecological value to the food forest. Many of these herbs serve dual purposes; they can be harvested for cooking and medicinal uses, while also playing vital ecological roles. Certain herbs repel pests naturally, reducing the need for chemical pesticides, and others attract pollinators. Plants like comfrey are particularly beneficial, as their deep taproots draw nutrients from deep within the soil. These nutrients can be accessed by surface plants when comfrey is cut and used as "chop-and-drop" mulch. This process supports soil health and fertility, providing an ongoing source of organic matter and essential nutrients.

At ground level, the ground cover layer consists of low-growing plants like clover, strawberries, creeping thyme, and oregano, which protect the soil from erosion and weed invasion. Ground covers function as living mulch, reducing soil moisture loss and suppressing unwanted plant growth. This layer is essential for conserving soil moisture, reducing evaporation, and creating a protective carpet over the soil that prevents erosion and protects soil organisms. The ground cover layer is vital for maintaining soil health, as it reduces the need for synthetic mulch and ensures that the soil is continuously protected and hydrated.

The vine layer adds a vertical dimension to the orchard-based food forest, with climbing plants such as grapevines, kiwi, passionfruit, and beans. Vines are unique in that they do not compete heavily for ground space, as they climb the trees and shrubs for support. This approach makes efficient use of vertical space without shading out other plants. Leguminous vines like beans also add nitrogen to the soil, further supporting the nutrient cycle and contributing to the productivity of the entire system. This layer enhances the food forest's yields, providing a source of additional fruits and vegetables in a small footprint.

Finally, the root layer includes nutrient-rich root vegetables and tubers like garlic, onions, carrots, radishes, and sweet potatoes. Root crops offer a harvest below the ground, enriching the diversity of food produced by the forest and providing an essential food source. These plants also contribute to soil health by aerating the soil and creating channels that allow for better water infiltration and root penetration. As root crops are harvested, they leave small openings in the soil, promoting aeration and creating pathways for soil organisms. This enhances nutrient exchange and supports the complex soil web necessary for a healthy, self-sustaining ecosystem.

Together, these seven layers form a cohesive system that mimics the resilience and productivity of a natural forest. Each layer plays a specific role, with plants interacting in mutually beneficial ways that enhance the overall health, biodiversity, and productivity of the food forest. By optimizing light, soil, and water use, the orchard-based food forest model creates a stable, self-sustaining ecosystem that yields a diverse array of foods while supporting wildlife, improving soil health, and minimizing the need for external inputs. This layered approach provides a model for sustainable food production that not only meets human needs but also contributes to ecological balance, making it a valuable and resilient agricultural system for the future.

Benefits of the Orchard-Based Food Forest Model

The orchard-based food forest model offers numerous benefits by merging the productivity of an orchard with the ecological balance of a food forest. One of its primary advantages is enhanced productivity and diversity. By incorporating multiple layers of vegetation, from the canopy of fruit and nut trees to ground cover and root crops, this system allows for a high density of food production in a compact area. This layering approach enables simultaneous yields from fruit and nut trees, berry shrubs, culinary and medicinal herbs, vegetables, and root crops, maximizing the use of both vertical and horizontal space. This diversity also leads to a broader harvest range, meeting various nutritional and practical needs while fostering a healthier ecosystem.

The model's design is self-sustaining and low-maintenance, reducing the need for external inputs and human intervention. Once established, an orchard-based food forest largely manages itself, with plants working in harmony to recycle nutrients, attract beneficial insects, and control pests. For example, nitrogen-fixing plants enrich the soil, while flowering herbs attract pollinators and beneficial predators, naturally reducing pest populations. This setup decreases the need for fertilizers and pesticides, minimizing labor and resource costs over time and making it ideal for sustainable food production.

Soil health and water retention are greatly enhanced within this system due to the presence of perennial plants and a living ground cover layer. Unlike annual crops that leave soil exposed and vulnerable, perennials and ground covers build organic matter continuously, preventing soil erosion and fostering soil structure. The roots of these plants help retain moisture, creating a more resilient and drought-tolerant system. As organic matter accumulates, the soil's water-holding capacity improves, reducing the need for irrigation and supporting the long-term fertility of the orchard. This is a key benefit, as healthier soil directly translates to stronger, more productive plants and a sustainable agricultural model.

Biodiversity and resilience are central benefits of the orchard-based food forest, as the diverse plant species create a balanced and interconnected ecosystem. A wide range of plants and animals supports natural checks and balances, making the system less vulnerable to disease outbreaks, pest infestations, and environmental stresses like drought or temperature fluctuations. This built-in resilience helps maintain the system's productivity even under adverse conditions, making it an attractive option for adapting to climate variability.

Finally, the orchard-based food forest contributes to long-term sustainability and environmental benefits, including carbon sequestration. As trees, shrubs, and plants grow, they capture and store carbon in their biomass and in the soil, reducing greenhouse gasses in the atmosphere. The accumulation of organic matter in the soil further sequesters carbon, making this model an effective tool in combating climate change. By combining food production with ecological stewardship, the orchard-based food forest model not only provides diverse, sustainable yields but also supports environmental health. Its multifunctional design captures the efficiency of natural systems, presenting a scalable, sustainable solution that meets human needs while preserving ecological balance and promoting a healthy future for both agriculture and the environment.. In summary, the orchard-based food forest model is an innovative approach that blends the productivity and structure of traditional orchards with the resilience and ecological benefits of food forests.

WOODLAND AND FOREST GARDENS

Woodland gardens are ecologically rich landscapes that replicate the structure and dynamics of natural forests while providing a range of edible and useful plants. Built on permaculture principles, these systems integrate multiple layers of vegetation in a way that minimizes maintenance, enhances biodiversity, and produces sustainable yields. Numerous case studies and samples from around the world have demonstrated the success of woodland gardens in various climates, showcasing their potential as models for sustainable agriculture, biodiversity conservation, and environmental restoration.

One of the most prominent illustrations of a woodland garden is the Martin Crawford Agroforestry Research Trust forest garden in Devon, England. Established in the early 1990s, this two-acre garden has become a well-known example of a productive, low-maintenance food forest. Crawford designed the garden with seven distinct layers: canopy trees, understory trees, shrubs, herbaceous plants, ground covers, vines, and root crops. His focus on creating a self-sustaining ecosystem has resulted in a thriving garden with over 500 species, including apples, pears, hazelnuts, currants, and perennial vegetables. Minimal maintenance is required as Crawford carefully selected plants that support each other through natural nutrient cycling and pest control. His garden serves as a model of how a carefully designed woodland system can yield food, timber, medicinal herbs, and wildlife habitat, all while restoring soil health and conserving water. The site is also a resource for research and education, offering visitors insights into agroforestry, forest gardening, and sustainable land use practices.

Another significant woodland garden model comes from Robert Hart, who pioneered temperate forest gardening in the United Kingdom. Starting his garden in the 1970s in Shropshire, England, Hart sought to develop a productive, ecologically balanced system that required minimal labor. He implemented a seven-layered approach, integrating a canopy layer of fruit and nut trees, an understory of smaller fruit trees, shrubs for berries and nitrogen fixation, herbaceous plants, ground covers, climbing vines, and root crops. Hart's garden produced a diverse range of fruits, nuts, herbs, and vegetables, all while fostering a resilient, disease-resistant environment. His model challenges the notion that forest gardening is feasible only in tropical climates and demonstrates the viability of temperate woodland gardens. Robert Hart's work has since inspired a generation of forest gardeners, reinforcing the idea that food forests can thrive in various climates by harnessing perennial plants and working with natural ecosystems.

The Edible Woodland Garden at the Occidental Arts and Ecology Center (OAEC) in California provides another instructive example, particularly for Mediterranean and semi-arid climates. This 25-acre woodland garden features a diverse mix of native plants and Mediterranean climate-adapted edibles like persimmons, figs, grapes, and berries. The OAEC woodland garden maximizes water retention through mulching and strategic plant selection to endure California's dry summers, proving that forest gardens can adapt to seasonal drought. With an emphasis on native plants, the OAEC garden supports local wildlife and conserves biodiversity while producing food. This model shows how woodland gardens can be adapted to the unique conditions of Mediterranean and arid climates, utilizing native species and resource-efficient practices.

In the United States, the Beacon Food Forest in Seattle, Washington, is a community-driven woodland garden project on public land that covers seven acres. The Beacon Food Forest combines food production with community engagement, education, and biodiversity conservation. It includes fruit and nut trees, berry bushes, edible perennials, and native plants arranged in a layered structure. Managed by volunteers, the garden provides free access to fresh produce, engages the local community, and serves as a green space in an urban setting. This project demonstrates how woodland gardens can be adapted to urban areas as shared resources, enhancing food security and community cohesion.

Ernst Götsch's syntropic agroforestry in Brazil is another compelling example, illustrating how woodland gardens can restore degraded lands. Götsch's method involves high-density planting, strategic pruning, and succession planting to create productive, self-sustaining forest gardens in tropical climates. His approach has turned degraded land into biodiverse forests that yield bananas, cocoa, cassava, and more. By focusing on soil health, water retention, and biodiversity, Götsch's forest gardens are resilient against pests, drought, and environmental stresses, serving as a model for regenerative agriculture in the tropics.

Other inspiring examples include the Mesoamerican forest gardens maintained by indigenous communities, which have existed for centuries. These gardens feature a mix of food crops, medicinal plants, and native trees that support the local ecosystem. Often referred to as "home gardens" or "milpas," these systems integrate a deep understanding of plant interactions and biodiversity. They demonstrate how traditional woodland gardening knowledge contributes to sustainable living, biodiversity, and food security while maintaining cultural heritage.

Each of these case studies illustrates the adaptability and versatility of woodland gardens, highlighting their potential in various climates, landscapes, and contexts. From the temperate gardens of the United Kingdom to the community-driven urban projects in Seattle and the regenerative tropical systems in Brazil, these woodland gardens showcase principles of low-maintenance, ecologically harmonious food production. Through careful design and plant selection, woodland gardens not only support biodiversity and ecosystem health but also offer sustainable solutions to food production, water conservation, and climate resilience. They demonstrate a pathway for integrating food systems within natural ecosystems, making them ideal models for future agricultural and urban planning.

CHAPTER NINE

DEVELOPING A MAINTENANCE PLAN

Developing a good maintenance plan for a food forest is crucial to ensuring long-term productivity, resilience, and ecological health. Unlike conventional gardens, food forests require minimal intervention once they are established, but a thoughtful approach to ongoing management helps support plant health, optimize yields, and prevent potential issues from disrupting the ecosystem. A strong maintenance plan addresses key factors such as soil health, plant pruning, weed control, pest management, and seasonal tasks. Below is a comprehensive guide to creating an effective maintenance plan for a food forest. The primary goal of maintaining a food forest is to support a self-sustaining system that mimics natural ecosystems while providing food, medicine, and other benefits. Maintenance efforts in a food forest are often aimed at encouraging plant diversity, promoting beneficial relationships between plants and animals, and creating conditions where plants can grow with minimal human intervention. A good maintenance plan focuses on promoting soil health, managing water resources, and supporting a balanced ecosystem that can adapt over time.

Soil health, water management, and plant care are foundational principles in food forest systems, each playing a crucial role in creating a resilient and productive ecosystem. Soil health is particularly important, as it provides the basis for plant growth, nutrient cycling, and the overall balance of the food forest. Instead of relying on synthetic fertilizers, food forests focus on natural practices that maintain and enhance the soil's fertility and structure, supporting a diverse range of plants and organisms. One key strategy is mulching, which involves applying a thick layer of organic materials—like leaf litter, straw, or wood chips—around the base of trees and plants. This layer helps conserve soil moisture, suppresses weeds, and returns organic matter as it decomposes, enriching the soil over time and encouraging beneficial microbial activity. Mulching materials break down slowly, ensuring a steady release of nutrients and creating a moist, hospitable environment for soil organisms that contribute to overall soil health.

The chop-and-drop method is another effective soil-building technique in food forests. This approach involves cutting back fast-growing, nitrogen-fixing plants like comfrey or clover and dropping the cuttings around trees or shrubs. As these cut plants decompose, they release nutrients into the soil, enriching it naturally without the need for external fertilizers. This technique not only provides nutrients but also helps build soil structure by adding organic matter that improves moisture retention and soil aeration. By using plants that grow quickly and fix nitrogen, the chop-and-drop method supports a regenerative cycle, where plants contribute to soil fertility in addition to their other ecological functions within the food forest. Cover cropping complements these soil health strategies by adding seasonal protection to the soil. Cover crops like clover, rye, or legumes are planted between the main layers, particularly in the winter. These crops prevent soil erosion, suppress weeds, and add organic matter as they decay. They can also fix nitrogen into the soil, boosting fertility for the next growing season. Finally, adding compost and natural fertilizers like seaweed or bone meal to the soil introduces essential nutrients and minerals, supporting soil life and improving its structure over time. These organic amendments not only feed plants directly but also nourish soil organisms, which play a vital role in nutrient cycling within the food forest ecosystem.

Water management is equally essential in a food forest, as adequate moisture is necessary for plants to thrive without relying on excessive irrigation. Passive water harvesting techniques, like using swales, berms, and rain gardens, are designed to capture rainwater and direct it to areas where it's most needed, minimizing water runoff and enhancing soil infiltration. These structures are especially beneficial in regions with dry climates or during periods of drought, as they help conserve water by storing it within the soil for slow release to plants. Passive water harvesting systems integrate seamlessly into the food forest landscape, reducing the need for artificial irrigation and allowing natural rainfall to support plant growth. When additional irrigation is needed, drip irrigation systems or soaker hoses can be used to deliver water directly to plant roots, minimizing water loss through evaporation and runoff. These systems target specific plants with precision, ensuring efficient use of water resources. Mulching and ground cover plants further support water retention in the soil, reducing the frequency and amount of irrigation needed by keeping the soil cool and moist. Together, these techniques create a self-sustaining water system that conserves resources while providing plants with the moisture they require.

Pruning and plant management are also key aspects of maintaining a healthy, productive food forest. Pruning allows gardeners to control plant size, shape, and density, improving air circulation and sunlight penetration, which in turn reduces disease risk and enhances productivity. For fruit and nut trees, pruning is essential to promote healthy growth, manage size, and remove dead or diseased branches, which supports better fruit production and tree health overall. Regular pruning helps fruit trees allocate energy toward producing higher-quality fruit rather than excessive foliage, leading to a more abundant and productive harvest. Shrubs and vines, such as berry bushes or nitrogen-fixing plants, also benefit from periodic trimming to encourage new growth, prevent overgrowth, and ensure that they remain within their designated areas. This control is important in a food forest to maintain balance and avoid overcrowding, which can disrupt airflow and sunlight access.

Herbs and ground cover plants, such as mint and thyme, require more frequent trimming to prevent them from becoming invasive or dominating nearby plants. Many herbs, like mint, have a tendency to spread aggressively if left unchecked, so periodic cutting back helps manage their growth while encouraging fresh, vigorous shoots. Pruning herbs not only keeps them manageable but also encourages them to produce new growth, resulting in more flavorful leaves and a prolonged harvest season. In addition, regularly trimming ground covers helps maintain an open understory layer, ensuring that other plants in the food forest can access nutrients and light without competition. Effective plant management keeps each layer of the food forest productive and in harmony with the others, contributing to an overall balance that supports the health of the entire ecosystem.

Weed control, pest management, and thoughtful harvesting play vital roles in maintaining a balanced and productive food forest, especially in the early stages when young plants are vulnerable. Effective weed management is essential to establish a strong foundation for the forest's growth, preventing aggressive species from outcompeting desired plants. A key strategy is the use of ground covers like clover, thyme, or creeping oregano, which create a dense, protective layer that inhibits weed germination while enriching the soil with nutrients. Ground covers serve a dual purpose by reducing competition and adding organic matter, gradually building soil health as they decompose and create a living mulch. Mulching is another crucial technique for weed suppression, as it not only helps prevent weeds but also conserves soil moisture, keeping roots cool and hydrated. By layering organic materials like straw, wood chips, or compost around plants, gardeners can reduce weed germination significantly, especially during the growing season. In cases where particularly persistent weeds or invasive plants are present, manual weeding may be necessary initially, though this need should decrease as ground covers and mulch layers become established.

Pest and disease management in a food forest relies on fostering a balanced ecosystem, where beneficial insects, birds, and other predators play a natural role in keeping pest populations under control. Diverse planting is a core practice, with various plant species chosen for their ability to attract pollinators and beneficial insects that feed on common pests. Herbs like dill, fennel, and marigold, for instance, attract predatory insects like ladybugs that help control aphids, while flowers provide habitat for other beneficial insects. By supporting this diversity, the food forest encourages a self-sustaining cycle, where pests are naturally regulated through predator-prey dynamics. Physical barriers, such as netting, are sometimes used to protect more sensitive plants, while manual removal of pests can be done in a targeted way to address small outbreaks without disrupting the balance of the ecosystem. Regular observation and early intervention are essential for managing both pests and diseases before they become problematic. Through routine monitoring, gardeners can spot signs of pest pressure or disease early, addressing them with natural remedies, such as insecticidal soaps or neem oil, only when necessary. This approach avoids the use of harsh chemicals and allows the food forest's natural resilience to develop over time.

Harvesting in a food forest requires a thoughtful approach to maintain plant health and biodiversity, focusing on rotation and interval-based harvesting. By rotating harvesting activities across different sections of the forest, gardeners prevent depletion in any one area, allowing plants to recover and regenerate. For example, fruit trees are typically harvested in late summer, while berry bushes yield crops throughout the growing season and herbs are collected as needed. This diversity in harvest timing and frequency ensures that no single plant or area is overtaxed, preserving the forest's productivity across the season. Furthermore, it's important to avoid stripping plants completely, especially perennials, to ensure they continue producing year after year. Selective harvesting of root crops, for instance, helps maintain soil stability and structure, which is vital for the health of surrounding plants and the ecosystem as a whole. This approach also allows plants to put energy into regrowth, supporting their ongoing vitality and contributing to the forest's resilience.

Long-term adaptation and planning are integral to sustaining a food forest as it matures. A food forest is a dynamic system that evolves over time, requiring ongoing assessment and adjustments to respond to changes in environmental conditions, plant performance, and the forest's structure. Seasonal monitoring allows gardeners to evaluate which plants are thriving and which may need extra support or replacement. Climate shifts, pest pressures, or other environmental changes can impact plant success, and being flexible with the plant palette is key to maintaining diversity and ecosystem stability. Introducing new species periodically helps keep the forest dynamic and adaptive, offering different ecological functions or filling new niches as they emerge. For example, adding plants that are more resilient to drought or changing temperature ranges can strengthen the forest against shifting climate conditions. Succession planning also plays a role as the forest's canopy matures and certain plants reach their full growth potential. This involves strategic pruning and thinning to make room for new growth, allowing younger plants, shrubs, and herbs to establish in spaces that open up. Natural succession is encouraged, with gardeners shaping the forest by allowing mature trees to develop, creating new opportunities for understory plants and fostering a continually evolving ecosystem.

Altogether, these interconnected strategies create a robust system that encourages natural processes and reduces human intervention. Weed management through ground covers and mulching, pest control by supporting beneficial species, and mindful harvesting routines help establish a self-sustaining, resilient food forest. By embracing a long-term perspective, monitoring plant health, adapting to environmental changes, and allowing natural succession, gardeners ensure the food forest continues to thrive, providing both ecological and harvestable benefits. Through this holistic approach, the food forest becomes a balanced ecosystem where plants, soil, insects, and wildlife work together, mirroring the processes of a natural forest while delivering a steady supply of food and resources. This method not only sustains the productivity of the food forest but also promotes biodiversity, strengthens resilience against pests and environmental changes, and fosters a rich, self-sustaining ecosystem.

SEASONAL TASKS AND OBSERVATIONS

A maintenance plan for a food forest requires thoughtful, seasonal tasks and regular observation, aligning with the natural rhythms of the ecosystem to ensure its health and productivity. By focusing on the specific needs of each season, gardeners can foster a resilient and self-sustaining food forest while also identifying and responding to potential issues as they arise. Seasonal tasks, such as planting, pruning, mulching, and monitoring for pests, not only help sustain the food forest's productivity but also support its long-term ecological stability. Observing how each plant interacts within the system over the year allows gardeners to make informed adjustments and gradually deepen their understanding of the forest's dynamics.

In spring, food forest maintenance is in full swing as the garden awakens from winter dormancy. This season involves foundational tasks such as planting new species, mulching, pruning, and applying soil amendments. New planting ensures that the food forest remains diverse and resilient; spring is an ideal time to introduce beneficial plants like nitrogen fixers, ground covers, and insect-attracting species that will enhance the ecosystem. Mulching helps retain moisture, moderate soil temperatures, and suppress weeds, giving new and existing plants a good start for the growing season. Pruning and cutting back overgrown plants also help manage growth, encourage fruiting, and improve air circulation to prevent diseases. Another critical aspect of spring is soil amendment application, which replenishes nutrients depleted over winter and supports vigorous growth. This is also a valuable time for observing the returning plants, assessing where gaps may exist, and noting if any plants need replacing. These observations help gardeners make timely decisions on plant health and density, ensuring that each layer in the food forest is well-represented and balanced.

Summer is a period of rapid growth and activity in the food forest, with tasks shifting toward water management, pest control, weeding, and harvesting. Since many plants are in their peak growing phase, ensuring consistent and efficient irrigation is crucial. Mulch applied earlier in spring assists in retaining moisture, but regular monitoring is necessary to prevent water stress in extreme heat. This season also demands vigilance regarding pests and diseases, as they are most active during warm weather. Gardeners can observe the forest's natural pest-management system in action, where beneficial insects, birds, and predator-prey dynamics help keep pest populations in check. However, some hand-picking of pests or targeted organic treatments may be necessary to support vulnerable plants. Another vital task in summer is weeding, as weeds compete with young and established plants for nutrients, water, and light. Managing weeds early and often keeps them from overshadowing more desirable species. Harvesting early crops like berries, herbs, and vegetables is also an important task, ensuring optimal flavor and preventing overripening or spoilage. Observing the pollinator activity during summer provides insight into the overall health of the ecosystem, as bees, butterflies, and other pollinators are essential for the food forest's productivity and biodiversity.

As the growing season winds down in fall, maintenance tasks focus on harvesting the remaining crops, preparing for winter, and reinforcing the forest's resilience. Fall harvesting often includes a variety of fruits, nuts, and vegetables, allowing gardeners to enjoy the food forest's bounty. Post-harvest pruning is essential to remove spent plant material, prevent disease, and prepare plants for the dormant season. Some plants, such as perennials, benefit from light pruning to reduce their height and create airflow, while others may require more substantial cuts to remove dead wood. This is also a good time to add a fresh layer of mulch to insulate soil, conserve moisture, and suppress cool-season weeds. Applying mulch in the fall protects plant roots from fluctuating winter temperatures, preventing frost damage and creating a stable environment for soil organisms. Additionally, fall is an ideal time for planting cover crops like clover, rye, or vetch. These crops enrich the soil by fixing nitrogen and adding organic matter when they decompose, preparing the soil for spring planting. Cover crops also provide ground cover, reducing erosion and weed growth over the winter months. Fall is a valuable time for making further observations on plant health, noting any potential issues to address in the upcoming season, and planning adjustments based on the year's growth patterns.

Winter in the food forest is a period of dormancy for most plants, and maintenance tasks are minimal. However, this season offers an opportunity for planning and preparing for the coming year. Observing the food forest's structural elements—such as the placement of trees, shrubs, and pathways—without the distraction of full foliage can reveal insights for layout improvements or plant replacement. Winter is also an appropriate time for any significant structural pruning, as many plants are dormant, minimizing stress on them. Pruning during this period encourages healthier growth in spring and allows gardeners to shape the structure of trees and shrubs effectively. The absence of active growth makes it easier to identify and remove weak branches or reshape plants that have outgrown their designated space. In addition to pruning, winter is an ideal time to review the successes and challenges of the past year, record observations, and make detailed plans for spring. Whether it's introducing new plant varieties, adjusting the layout for better sun exposure, or refining the mulching schedule, winter planning ensures a smoother transition into the busy spring season.

A seasonal maintenance plan is essential for a thriving food forest because it aligns with natural cycles and enables gardeners to proactively address the unique needs of each period. The cyclical nature of food forests means that the actions taken in one season often have lasting effects on the subsequent ones, making timely, seasonal tasks critical for sustainable management. Observations from each season accumulate into a deeper understanding of the food forest's ecosystem, allowing for more informed and intuitive decision-making over time. By following a seasonal plan that includes planting, mulching, pruning, water management, pest control, soil enrichment, and winter planning, gardeners can create a food forest that is not only productive but also self-sustaining and ecologically balanced. This method of attentive, seasonally adjusted maintenance transforms a food forest from a simple collection of plants into a dynamic, interconnected ecosystem that provides abundant food, nurtures biodiversity, and aligns with the rhythms of nature.

NO TILL GARDENING

No-till gardening is a regenerative approach to managing soil that avoids disturbing the soil structure by digging or plowing. In a food forest, no-till gardening works exceptionally well because it aligns with the principles of forest ecosystems, where organic matter builds up on the forest floor, creating rich, fertile soil without any human interference. Implementing no-till gardening in a food forest supports soil health, water retention, biodiversity, and productivity, making it a sustainable and low-maintenance choice.

What No-Till Gardening Is

No-till gardening is based on preserving the soil's natural structure and its intricate web of beneficial organisms. When soil is tilled, the delicate ecosystem within the soil—fungi, bacteria, earthworms, and other organisms—is disrupted, often resulting in compaction, erosion, and loss of organic matter. In a no-till system, soil layers are kept intact, and organic materials are added on top to allow natural processes to enrich and aerate the soil. This approach reduces the need for fertilizers, conserves moisture, improves plant resilience, and prevents the leaching of nutrients.

Additionally, no-till gardening in a food forest encourages healthy root growth, prevents weed growth, and fosters soil carbon sequestration.

Benefits of No-Till Gardening in a Food Forest

1. Soil Health: By preserving soil structure, no-till gardening allows beneficial fungi, bacteria, and microorganisms to thrive. These organisms help break down organic matter, recycle nutrients, and form symbiotic relationships with plant roots.

2. Water Retention: The undisturbed soil structure and added organic matter help improve water-holding capacity, reducing the need for frequent irrigation and helping plants survive dry spells.

3. Nutrient Cycling: Mulching and organic layering introduce nutrients into the soil naturally, as decomposing matter provides a steady supply of nitrogen, phosphorus, and potassium over time.

4. Reduced Weed Growth: Layers of organic matter inhibit weed seed germination, which reduces the need for weeding. Over time, many weeds are outcompeted by more robust ground covers.

5. Carbon Sequestration: No-till practices promote the storage of carbon within the soil by preserving root systems and adding organic materials that lock carbon away.

Implementing No-Till Gardening in a Food Forest

To create a no-till system in a food forest, follow these key steps to establish and maintain healthy soil and resilient plant layers:

Preparing the Site without Tilling

If starting from scratch or preparing a new area within an existing food forest, create planting zones without disturbing the soil. A common approach is **sheet mulching**, which involves layering organic materials directly on top of existing soil to build a fertile base for planting. Here's how:

- Lay down a layer of cardboard or thick newspaper over the soil. This layer will block light to suppress existing weeds and grasses while decomposing over time.
- Add a 6-12 inch layer of organic materials such as compost, aged manure, straw, leaves, and grass clippings on top. These materials break down and nourish the soil over time.
- Water each layer thoroughly to encourage decomposition and promote microbial activity.
- Leave the mulched area to settle for a few weeks, if possible, before planting.

Establishing Layers of Mulch and Organic Matter

In a food forest, maintaining a natural, layered structure helps mimic the organic matter build-up that occurs in natural forests. Layer organic materials seasonally:

- Apply mulch regularly: Use materials such as wood chips, straw, and leaf litter around the base of trees, shrubs, and perennial plants. Mulch conserves moisture, suppresses weeds, and provides habitat for beneficial soil organisms.
- Add compost and organic material periodically: Adding a layer of compost or aged manure around plants every season nourishes the

soil. Organic material like compost also helps improve the soil's texture and nutrient content.

- Incorporate "chop-and-drop" plants: Plant nitrogen-fixing species, such as clover, comfrey, or legumes, and periodically cut them back, dropping the trimmings around trees and shrubs as green mulch. This "chop-and-drop" method adds nutrients and supports the natural nutrient cycle.

Building and Maintaining Soil Fertility with Cover Crops

In between food-producing plants or layers, cover crops like clover, vetch, or buckwheat can be planted to fix nitrogen, improve soil structure, and suppress weeds. These crops are often grown, then "cut and dropped" onto the ground, providing a green mulch layer that decomposes into the soil. Over time, the roots of cover crops improve aeration, break up compacted soil, and create channels for water infiltration.

Minimizing Soil Disturbance When Planting

When adding new plants or transplanting in a no-till food forest, try to disturb the soil as little as possible:

- Dig only small holes for each plant, just enough to fit the root system.
- Avoid large-scale digging or disturbing the soil around established plants. Instead, add new layers of mulch or compost around plants to encourage new growth without disrupting existing roots and soil life.
- For large trees or shrubs, use a broadfork if necessary to gently loosen the soil rather than turning it over, preserving the soil structure while creating space for planting.

Supporting Soil Health through Biodiversity

Promote biodiversity within the food forest to encourage a naturally balanced ecosystem:

- Plant a wide variety of species in layers, including trees, shrubs, herbs, ground covers, and vines, to create a resilient ecosystem that supports soil health and reduces the need for intervention.
- Include companion plants that support each other. For example, nitrogen-fixing plants, pollinator attractors, and pest repellents help maintain soil quality and balance the ecosystem without disrupting the soil.
- Create natural edges and pathways to reduce soil compaction from foot traffic in growing areas.

Long-Term Soil Building through Decomposition

Maintaining a no-till food forest involves layering organic materials seasonally and allowing natural processes of decomposition to build soil fertility over time. The natural decomposition process allows fungi, bacteria, earthworms, and other organisms to break down organic material gradually, which helps create rich, loamy soil that continues to nourish plants.

Maintaining a No-Till System in the Food Forest

Once the no-till system is established, it requires only periodic maintenance to keep the layers healthy and productive:

- Refresh mulch and organic layers as needed**: Add new mulch and compost seasonally, especially around the base of trees and plants.
- Observe and adapt: Regularly check the soil's health by observing plant growth and soil texture. If areas look compacted, avoid digging; instead, add another layer of organic material or plant cover crops to improve aeration.
- Monitor plant health: Ensure that your plants are thriving, which indicates that the soil is fertile and balanced. If plants show signs of nutrient deficiency, add compost or an organic fertilizer that can enrich the soil without disrupting the no-till approach.

CHAPTER TEN

HARVESTING AND PRESERVATION

HARVESTING

Harvesting crops in a food forest requires techniques that accommodate the variety of plants and mimic natural ecosystems. Since food forests are typically polycultures with multiple layers of plants, the approach to harvesting is strategic, ensuring minimal disturbance and maintaining plant health. Different crops, from fruit trees and shrubs to herbs, root vegetables, and ground covers, each require specific techniques that align with the food forest's low-maintenance philosophy.

Fruit and Nut Trees (Canopy and Understory Layers)

In a food forest, fruit and nut trees make up the essential canopy and understory layers, providing an abundant supply of seasonal produce and supporting the ecosystem's diversity and productivity. Harvesting these trees involves different techniques tailored to the tree size and fruit type, ensuring both efficiency and the health of the plants. Larger fruit trees, such as apples, pears, and plums, require careful handling to avoid damaging their branches. Using a fruit-picking pole with a basket is highly effective, as it allows easy access to higher branches without the need to climb, which can be unsafe and harmful to the tree. Gently twisting the fruit to remove it, rather than pulling, prevents tearing the branch, which could otherwise introduce disease or hinder future growth. Additionally, fallen fruit should be collected promptly to deter pests like rodents and insects, which are attracted to decaying produce. Clearing fallen fruit also keeps the ground clean, making it easier to monitor the area and manage pest populations effectively.

Nut trees, such as chestnuts, walnuts, and almonds, have different harvesting requirements, as nuts typically reach maturity when they naturally fall to the ground. Gathering them after they drop is a simple, low-impact method that aligns with the trees' natural cycle. However, during peak ripening, some growers may also gently shake branches to release nuts, particularly in large-scale harvests. Regular ground inspection is vital in preventing wildlife from depleting the yield before it can be harvested, as animals are naturally drawn to nuts during ripening. By keeping a consistent harvesting schedule, food forest managers can secure the nut crop efficiently while maintaining a healthy balance with local wildlife.

Dwarf or smaller fruit trees, including varieties like pawpaw, fig, and elderberry, provide easier access to fruit, as their shorter stature makes them suitable for hand-picking. These trees are popular in food forests for their high yield and manageable size, which allows for straightforward harvest and maintenance. Due to the delicate nature of fruits like figs and elderberries, which can bruise or spoil easily, it's essential to handle them with care. Gently twisting the fruit from the stem and placing it directly into a padded container helps preserve its quality by preventing bruising. Harvesting smaller fruit trees often requires more frequent collection, as these fruits are more susceptible to ripening quickly, which can attract pests if left on the tree or ground too long.

Beyond harvesting, fruit and nut trees play a critical role in the food forest's overall health by contributing organic matter and creating microhabitats for beneficial insects and birds. Canopy and understory trees regulate the light that filters down to lower layers, providing shade for shade-tolerant plants and helping retain moisture in the soil, essential for healthy ground cover. Fallen leaves from these trees add organic matter, nourishing the soil and supporting nutrient cycles that benefit the entire forest. As these trees mature, they also offer increased stability to the ecosystem, as their deep root systems aid in erosion control and enhance water retention in the soil.

By maintaining regular harvesting practices and understanding the specific needs of fruit and nut trees, a food forest can continue to thrive, producing high yields with minimal disruption to the natural environment. The combination of careful harvesting techniques, wildlife-friendly practices, and ecological benefits solidifies the role of canopy and understory trees as cornerstones in a resilient, sustainable food forest. Their productive and structural contributions help establish a balanced ecosystem that supports diverse plant and animal life, creating a self-sustaining, regenerative landscape.

Berry Bushes and Shrubs (Shrub Layer)

Berry bushes and shrubs, which form the essential shrub layer in a food forest, are both productive and integral to the ecosystem. Berries like blueberries, raspberries, blackberries, and currants are commonly grown in food forests because they yield abundant harvests and attract pollinators and beneficial wildlife. Harvesting these berries requires careful timing and technique, as berries are most flavorful and nutritious when fully ripe and do not continue ripening once picked. Hand-harvesting is ideal, as it allows for a gentle touch to avoid damaging the fruit and plant. The best way to pick berries is by cupping the fruit and applying a light pull; ripe berries will release easily, while unripe ones will resist, signaling they need more time on the plant. This method helps ensure that only mature, ready-to-eat berries are collected.

Maintaining the health of berry bushes involves a balanced approach to harvesting. It's beneficial not to strip the bush entirely of its fruit; leaving a few berries behind serves several purposes. These leftover fruits provide food for local wildlife, such as birds and small mammals, which are natural contributors to seed dispersal in the forest. By consuming and spreading seeds, these animals help propagate new plants, supporting the diversity and resilience of the food forest. Additionally, the presence of some ripe berries encourages pollinators, as they are attracted to the vibrant colors and sweet scent of mature fruit. This cycle of pollination and dispersal reinforces the ecological health of the area and aids in maintaining a balanced ecosystem where plants, insects, and animals coexist in harmony.

Leaving a few berries on the bushes also has direct benefits for the plant itself. This practice can reduce the physiological stress on the plant by ensuring it doesn't expend all its energy in a single harvest season. Rather, the plant can gradually focus on new growth and preparing for the next productive cycle. Regular, modest harvesting helps to boost the plant's resilience, encouraging more vigorous growth and higher yields in future seasons. In fact, by allowing a natural cycle of growth and regeneration, berry bushes can become more robust over time, developing deeper roots and more extensive canopies that contribute to soil stability and moisture retention in the shrub layer.

Herbs and Medicinal Plants (Herbaceous Layer)
Herbs such as mint, thyme, sage, and basil are best harvested by **pinching off leaves or stems** in the morning after the dew has dried, as this is when the essential oils are most concentrated. For herbs like comfrey, which are used in "chop-and-drop" mulching, **cut back the entire plant at the base** and spread the leaves around other plants as natural mulch.

Many herbs can be harvested throughout the season with a technique called "cut and come again." This involves harvesting only the top third of the plant, which allows it to continue producing. Frequent, moderate harvesting encourages bushier growth, keeping the herbs productive throughout the season. If collecting seeds from plants like dill or fennel, wait until the seeds are dry and brown, then shake them into a bag for collection.

Ground Cover Crops (Ground Cover Layer)
Ground covers like clover, strawberries, and creeping thyme provide soil cover, weed suppression, and food. **Harvesting ground covers** such as strawberries requires gentle picking of the ripe fruit, ideally in the morning when they are firm. Harvest only the fully ripe strawberries by pinching the stem above the berry to avoid damaging the plant.

For ground covers like clover, which are used for nitrogen-fixing rather than food production, consider a "chop-and-drop" technique. Periodically cut clover back with shears, letting the trimmings decompose on the soil as green mulch, which adds nutrients and promotes a healthy soil structure.

Vines (Vine Layer)
Vines like grapes, kiwi, and passionfruit utilize the vertical space in a food forest and often require **trellising or support**. To harvest these, wait until the fruit reaches full ripeness. Grapes, for instance, should be clipped in whole clusters using scissors or shears to avoid damaging the vine.

For legumes like pole beans, hand-pick beans when they reach the desired size. Regular harvesting encourages further production and prevents the vine from diverting energy to seed development. Check vines regularly and gently pluck fruits without yanking, which could damage the vine or dislodge nearby plants.

Root Vegetables and Tubers (Root Layer)
Root vegetables like carrots, onions, garlic, and tubers like sweet potatoes are generally harvested by hand-digging around the plant base. Use a garden fork or a small hand trowel to loosen the soil around the roots, being careful not to pierce or bruise them.

For garlic and onions, harvest when the leaves begin to yellow and fall over. Carefully dig under the bulb to lift it out, then let it cure in a dry, shaded area to enhance flavor and longevity. For tubers like sweet potatoes, wait until the vines start to die back, indicating maturity. Dig carefully around the tuber's base, gently lifting each root to avoid damage.

Perennial Vegetables

In a food forest, perennial vegetables like asparagus, rhubarb, and artichoke add diversity to the yield. For asparagus, harvest young shoots in spring by cutting them at ground level when they are about 6–8 inches tall. With rhubarb, pull stalks away from the plant base rather than cutting, which helps it regrow. Avoid over-harvesting perennials to maintain their longevity and productivity.

Seed Harvesting for Propagation

For plants grown for both food and propagation, allow some crops to go to seed for collection. Harvesting seeds can support the food forest's expansion and long-term resilience. Allow herbs, annuals, or even some vegetables to flower and dry on the plant before collecting seeds. Store seeds in a dry, cool place for the next planting cycle, contributing to a sustainable, self-sufficient forest system.

Practicing selective, moderate harvesting is essential to maintaining a balanced food forest. By focusing on seasonal and successive harvesting, you can gather ripe produce throughout the year without depleting any single plant or layer. Rotating harvest areas helps maintain plant vigor, reduces soil compaction, and supports wildlife. Additionally, maintain pathways to access plants easily and avoid stepping on planting areas, which could damage root systems and compact soil.

FOOD PRESERVATION

Food preservation is a critical part of extending the life of harvested crops, especially in a food forest where yields can vary throughout the year. Proper preservation methods like drying, canning, and freezing ensure that food remains safe, nutritious, and flavorful for months or even years. Each method has unique benefits, challenges, and applications, making it essential to understand how each works to maximize the shelf-life and quality of different foods.

Drying

Drying is one of the oldest methods of food preservation, utilizing heat and airflow to remove moisture from food, which prevents bacterial growth and spoilage. There are various drying techniques, from sun drying and air drying to more modern methods like using a dehydrator or an oven. This method is effective for fruits, vegetables, herbs, and even meats in the form of jerky.

Types of Drying

- Sun Drying: This method works best in hot, dry climates with plenty of sunlight and low humidity. Thinly sliced fruits or herbs are laid out on trays or racks and covered with mesh to keep insects away. Sun drying can take several days and requires consistently dry weather.

- Air Drying: Used mostly for herbs and flowers, air drying involves hanging bundles in a well-ventilated, warm area out of direct sunlight. The airflow helps evaporate moisture without the need for additional heat.

- Dehydrators: Food dehydrators provide a consistent, controlled heat source and airflow, speeding up the drying process. They are particularly useful for high-moisture foods like tomatoes or apples, allowing drying times of only a few hours.

- Oven Drying: An oven set to a low temperature (around 140°F or 60°C) can mimic the effects of a dehydrator. Food is arranged on trays and turned periodically to ensure even drying. Oven drying is more accessible for those without a dehydrator, though it can be less energy efficient.

Benefits of Drying

Dried foods offer a range of benefits, particularly in terms of space efficiency, shelf stability, and nutrient retention. Because drying removes most of the moisture from food, it not only reduces the weight and volume of the food, making it lightweight and compact for storage, but it also creates an inhospitable environment for bacteria and molds. This drying process makes foods highly shelf-stable, which means they can last for months or even years when stored properly. A cool, dark place is ideal, and airtight containers prevent exposure to air and moisture that can spoil the food. Dried foods can therefore remain a reliable food source well beyond the typical shelf life of fresh produce, offering a convenient way to preserve seasonal harvests for long-term use.

Nutritionally, drying preserves many essential nutrients, though some water-soluble vitamins like vitamin C can degrade in the drying process. However, a significant amount of the food's original nutritional value remains intact, making dried foods nutritionally dense and often concentrated in flavor. For this reason, dried fruits, herbs, and vegetables can be potent in both taste and health benefits, providing a viable and healthy alternative to fresh or frozen food options.

However, effective preservation requires careful attention to storage methods, as dried foods are susceptible to reabsorbing moisture from the air. If they do, they can develop mold and spoil, undermining the drying effort. To maintain quality, desiccant packets, which absorb moisture, can be added to storage containers, or vacuum-sealed bags can be used to ensure an airtight seal. Additionally, some foods benefit from pre-treatment before drying; blanching, a quick exposure to boiling water, helps retain color and texture and can prevent certain enzymes from breaking down the food's quality over time. Blanching is especially helpful with vegetables, as it stops the enzymatic activity that can affect flavor, color, and texture during storage.

Overall, drying food is a versatile and effective method of preservation, combining durability with nutritional benefits and flavor retention. Whether preparing for the off-season or preserving a harvest surplus, drying provides an efficient, long-lasting solution, especially when storage practices are managed to retain quality and minimize spoilage.

Canning

Canning is a preservation technique that involves placing food in jars or cans, then heating it to destroy bacteria and enzymes that cause spoilage. As the jar cools, a vacuum seal forms, preventing re-contamination. There are two primary methods of canning: water bath canning and pressure canning, each suited to different types of food.

Types of Canning

- Water Bath Canning: This method involves submerging jars in boiling water for a set period. It is suitable for high-acid foods like fruits, jams, jellies, pickles, and tomatoes (with added acid). High acidity naturally prevents bacterial growth, so the boiling water provides sufficient heat to ensure food safety.
- Pressure Canning: Low-acid foods like vegetables, meats, and soups require higher temperatures to kill bacteria like Clostridium botulinum, which can survive boiling temperatures. A pressure canner heats jars to 240°F (116°C), ensuring complete sterilization. This method is essential for low-acid foods and requires a specialized pressure canning unit.

Benefits of Canning

Canning is a reliable and versatile method for preserving food, offering extended shelf life, the preservation of flavors and textures, and a variety of food options that can be safely stored long-term. Properly canned foods can remain safe and edible for years, which makes canning an ideal solution for long-term storage and food security. Unlike other preservation methods, canning retains the food's natural flavors and, to some extent, its texture, allowing jams, pickles, sauces, and even soups to maintain their quality over time. This preservation of taste is particularly beneficial for foods like fruit preserves and pickled vegetables, where flavor is a key part of their appeal. Canning also offers flexibility, allowing a wide variety of foods to be preserved, from fruits and vegetables to meats and stews, making it highly adaptable to different harvests and dietary needs.

However, canning requires close attention to safety guidelines, as it involves sterilizing food in jars to prevent bacterial contamination, particularly for low-acid foods. If improperly processed, canned foods can develop botulism, a rare but serious foodborne illness. Therefore, it is essential to follow recommended guidelines for processing times and temperatures, particularly for low-acid foods that require pressure canning to reach temperatures high enough to ensure safety. High-acid foods, like fruits and pickles, can typically be safely canned with a simpler water bath method.

Storage considerations are also important. Canned goods need to be kept in a cool, dark space to ensure that the food remains stable and to prevent degradation of quality. This storage requirement can take up significant space, as jars must be safely stacked and labeled for easy access. An organized storage system can improve efficiency, making it easier to keep track of the canning inventory and use older items first to maintain freshness.

Additionally, while canning requires an initial investment in equipment, including jars, lids, and a canner, this setup can be used for many years. Jars and canning tools are reusable, meaning that after the initial costs, canning becomes a cost-effective preservation method over time. This makes canning a sustainable and worthwhile investment for those looking to preserve large amounts of food or maintain a steady, homemade food supply throughout the year. The benefits of long-lasting, flavor-rich, and varied canned goods make this preservation method particularly valuable for those interested in self-sufficiency and reducing food waste.

Freezing

Freezing is a modern preservation method that works by slowing down enzyme activity and bacterial growth at low temperatures. Foods are typically frozen shortly after harvest, retaining much of their nutritional content, color, and flavor. Freezing works well for most fruits, vegetables, meats, and prepared foods.

Types of Freezing

- Flash Freezing**: This involves freezing individual pieces of food on a tray before transferring them to a container. Flash freezing prevents pieces from clumping together and makes it easier to use small portions at a time. This technique is useful for berries, sliced fruits, and vegetables.
- Blanching Before Freezing: For vegetables, blanching (briefly boiling then cooling them) before freezing is recommended. Blanching deactivates enzymes that can cause flavor and texture changes, resulting in higher-quality frozen vegetables.
- Vacuum Sealing: Vacuum-sealing food before freezing removes air, which helps prevent freezer burn and preserves flavor and texture.

Benefits of Freezing

Freezing is an efficient preservation method that retains high nutritional value, offers convenience in meal preparation, and provides versatile storage options. Foods frozen soon after harvest retain most of their vitamins, minerals, and antioxidants, preserving their original nutritional profile. This is especially true when foods are frozen rapidly, as this process minimizes nutrient loss that can occur with other preservation methods. Frozen foods are also highly convenient; they can be cooked directly from the freezer without the need for thawing, saving time and making them a practical option for quick meal preparation. This aspect is especially useful for busy households, as frozen produce, meats, and prepared meals are ready to incorporate directly into recipes.

The versatility of freezing is another significant advantage, as it works well for a wide range of foods, from fruits and vegetables to complete meals, sauces, and broths. This flexibility means that freezing can adapt to whatever is available in the garden or local market, allowing for a varied and diverse stock of preserved foods. This adaptability makes freezing a particularly valuable tool for preserving seasonal produce, ensuring access to nutrient-rich foods year-round.

However, freezing does come with certain considerations, particularly in terms of storage and space. Freezers have limited capacity, and large harvests can quickly occupy significant space, which may be challenging to manage in a standard household freezer. Organizing and labeling are essential to make efficient use of freezer space and to avoid overstocking or losing track of stored items. Additionally, frozen foods require continuous electricity to maintain their preserved state, so reliable energy access is crucial. Power outages or lack of access to electricity can compromise frozen foods, posing a risk for those who rely heavily on this preservation method. For areas with inconsistent energy supply, freezing may not be the most sustainable option, as foods can spoil if power is lost for an extended period.

Quality can also be an issue over time, as freezer burn may develop on foods stored for long periods or in non-airtight containers. Freezer burn occurs when moisture in the food evaporates, leading to dry spots and changes in texture and flavor. Although freezer-burned food is safe to eat, it may lose some of its original appeal. To prevent freezer burn, proper packaging—such as using airtight containers or freezer-safe bags—is essential for preserving the quality of frozen foods over time.

Overall, freezing is a practical and nutrient-preserving method that offers quick access to a diverse range of foods. With proper management of storage space and packaging, freezing can be an excellent method to extend the life of foods while maintaining much of their original quality and nutritional value.

Choosing the Best Method

Choosing between drying, canning, and freezing for food preservation largely depends on the type of food, available resources, and the intended storage duration. Each method offers unique benefits, making it suitable for specific purposes and foods. Drying, for instance, is particularly effective for long-term storage in a compact, lightweight form and is ideal for herbs, fruits, and some vegetables. Because it removes most of the moisture, drying significantly reduces the risk of spoilage while retaining many of the food's nutrients. This makes dried foods not only space-efficient but also shelf-stable for extended periods when stored correctly, making them a reliable option for preserving small items and flavors for later use.

Canning is a preferred method for high-acid foods such as fruits and pickled vegetables, as well as foods that can be enjoyed in a preserved form, like jams, sauces, and soups. Canning seals foods in airtight jars through heat processing, which not only keeps them shelf-stable for years but also preserves much of their flavor and texture. For those interested in maintaining a ready-to-eat pantry of preserved produce, canning is a versatile choice. However, it requires an initial investment in equipment and careful adherence to safety protocols, particularly for low-acid foods, to prevent foodborne illnesses. This method works well for items that are intended to be stored long-term and can be used directly in prepared forms, such as soups or pasta sauces.

Freezing, on the other hand, is often the simplest preservation method and works well for a wide variety of produce, including fruits, vegetables, and prepared dishes. Freezing helps retain the fresh taste, color, and texture of foods and is especially useful when the goal is to preserve the food in its most natural state. Although it requires sufficient freezer space and consistent electricity, freezing allows for the preservation of foods quickly and with minimal processing. It's a great option for storing surplus produce that can be thawed and used later in recipes without significant changes in taste or nutritional value.

For those managing a food forest with abundant seasonal harvests, combining drying, canning, and freezing provides a flexible and comprehensive preservation strategy. By diversifying methods, it's possible to maximize the lifespan and quality of various foods, reduce waste, and ensure a steady supply of preserved produce throughout the year. For instance herbs and fruits might be dried, tomatoes canned into sauces, and fresh berries frozen to enjoy later. Together, these methods create a well-rounded approach to food security, allowing for adaptable, long-lasting, and varied food storage.

CONCLUSION

In conclusion, a food forest represents a profound synthesis of ecological wisdom, self-reliance, and sustainable living. The concepts and practices involved—from understanding natural succession to designing complex, multi-layered plant systems—are a testament to humanity's capacity to work in harmony with nature. As we have explored in this food forest guide, developing a food forest is more than simply planting trees and expecting results; it is about engaging deeply with the land, learning from its rhythms, and designing spaces that mimic the resilience, productivity, and diversity of natural ecosystems. Whether you are a seasoned gardener, a novice grower, or simply someone interested in a sustainable food system, establishing a food forest has the potential to transform the way you live and interact with the earth.

One of the core principles of a food forest is the idea of layering, where each layer serves a distinct function and contributes to the health of the overall system. From the towering canopy of fruit and nut trees to the ground covers, herbs, vines, and root layers, each element of a food forest works synergistically, creating a self-sustaining ecosystem that maximizes productivity while reducing the need for constant human intervention. The food forest model allows us to maximize the space we have and make full use of the resources nature provides, capturing sunlight, storing water, and recycling nutrients within a system that is both beautiful and functional.

Food forests also provide a unique opportunity to deepen our understanding of natural processes and to cultivate a landscape that supports not just human needs but those of countless other species. In a world where biodiversity is increasingly under threat, food forests stand as resilient sanctuaries for pollinators, birds, beneficial insects, and microorganisms. Each element plays a role in a delicate web of interactions that strengthens the forest as a whole, creating a stable and balanced environment. The diversity within a food forest is a vital asset, providing resilience against disease, pests, and climate variability, and building soil health over time. Through careful observation and thoughtful design, we can develop food forests that are well adapted to local conditions, making them sustainable and productive with minimal inputs.

In the process of building a food forest, we are also engaging in practices that benefit the climate and environment on a larger scale. Trees, shrubs, and perennial plants sequester carbon, helping to mitigate the impacts of climate change. The living soil, rich in organic matter and teeming with microorganisms, acts as a carbon sink, storing carbon in a way that enhances soil fertility and promotes healthy plant growth. By opting for a regenerative approach to land management, food forests contribute to healing the land, reducing soil erosion, and enhancing the water cycle. These practices align with a broader movement toward regenerative agriculture, offering solutions for both food security and ecological restoration.

Creating a food forest is, however, not without its challenges. It requires a commitment to learning and an understanding that success in a food forest is gradual and cumulative, often taking years to reach its full potential. Unlike traditional annual agriculture, where results are immediate, food forests require patience, adaptability, and a willingness to work with nature's slower rhythms. But this investment of time and effort is rewarded with a food system that becomes more resilient and productive over time, offering an abundance of harvests with less labor and fewer inputs. This long-term view encourages us to cultivate a relationship with the land that is not about extraction but about nurturing and stewardship, building a legacy that will benefit generations to come.

Furthermore, food forests offer an approach to food security that is rooted in self-sufficiency and resilience. By cultivating a diverse array of edible plants that fruit and ripen at different times, food forests provide a continuous supply of food that is not dependent on external inputs or global supply chains. This model of localized, self-reliant food production becomes particularly relevant in times of economic uncertainty or disruptions in conventional food systems. With a well-established food forest, communities and families have a reliable source of nutrition that fosters independence and empowers them to take control of their food supply.

From a personal perspective, creating a food forest also has transformative effects on our well-being. Working with the land provides a deep sense of purpose and fulfillment, grounding us in the rhythms of the seasons and giving us a chance to connect with the earth in a meaningful way. Planting, nurturing, and harvesting in a food forest can be a meditative experience, reminding us of our place within a greater web of life. As stewards of these ecosystems, we cultivate not only food but also gratitude, patience, and a sense of interconnectedness with nature.

Education and community involvement are key to the food forest movement's growth and impact. The principles and practices laid out in this guide are only the beginning; sharing knowledge, learning from others, and fostering community gardens and food forests allow these ideas to take root in neighborhoods, schools, and public spaces. When communities come together to build and maintain food forests, they create resilient local food systems and promote environmental awareness, intergenerational learning and social cohesion. Each food forest becomes a living example of what's possible when we embrace sustainable practices and take responsibility for our impact on the earth.

In closing, the journey of creating a food forest is one of profound transformation, both for the land and for those who steward it. This guide serves as a foundation, providing tools, techniques, and inspiration to start and maintain a food forest. But it is ultimately through hands-on experience, experimentation, and observation that the true wisdom of a food forest emerges. By committing to this path, we join a legacy of regenerative land management that has the power to revitalize ecosystems, nourish communities, and build a more sustainable future. May your food forest flourish, and may it inspire others to embark on their own journey of ecological stewardship and abundance.

This food forest Bible is a call to action, an invitation to cultivate spaces that feed our bodies, restore our land, and nurture our spirits. Whether you are just beginning or are well on your way, remember that every seed planted, every tree nurtured, and every ecosystem restored is a step toward a better world.

www.ingramcontent.com/pod-product-compliance
Lightning Source LLC
Chambersburg PA
CBHW052237100225
21751CB00008B/306